Poetic Lives:
Keats

Poetic Lives:
Keats

Robert Mighall

ET REMOTISSIMA PROPE

Poetic Lives
Published by Hesperus Press Limited
4 Rickett Street, London sw6 1RU
www.hesperuspress.com

First published by Hesperus Press Limited, 2009

Designed and typeset by Fraser Muggeridge studio
Printed in Jordan by Jordan National Press

ISBN: 978-1-84391-302-3

Contents

Sonnet
The Human Seasons

Four seasons fill the measure of the year;
* There are four seasons in the mind of man:*
He has his lusty Spring, when fancy clear
* Takes in all beauty with an easy span:*
He has his Summer, when luxuriously
* Spring's honied cud of youthful thought he loves*
To ruminate, and by such dreaming nigh
* His nearest unto heaven: quiet coves*
His soul has in its Autumn, when his wings
* He furleth close; contented so to look*
On mists in idleness – to let fair things
* Pass by unheeded as a threshold brook.*
He has his Winter too of pale misfeature,
Or else he would forego his mortal nature.

A Grave in Rome

In the most remote part of what is known as the 'Protestant Cemetery' to the south of Rome stands a grave with a curious inscription:

> This Grave contains all that was Mortal, of a young English Poet Who, on his Death Bed in the Bitterness of his heart at the Malicious Power of his enemies, Desired these Words to be engraven on his Tomb Stone.
>
> Here lies One Whose Name was writ in Water.

The poet is not named. For when he was interred here, at dawn on 26th February 1821, with just a few mourners to see him confined to this lonely plot, it seemed likely that the inscription would prove accurate. The reference to the poet's 'enemies' was added by well-meaning friends to the simple epitaph he had requested, and reflects their bitterness at how the literary world had ridiculed his efforts. He had aspired to achieve so much – no less than to be 'among the English poets'. But his final wish, as he dragged what he termed his 'posthumous existence' through the last agonising stages of tuberculosis, was for oblivion. He died aged twenty-five with the ambitions he had set himself un-fulfilled, and little reason to believe this was anything but the last word on a promising life cut short.

But the poet's grave no longer stands alone and anonymous. In 1881 the remains of Joseph Severn, who had accompanied the poet to Rome sixty years before, were laid next to him, and a similar stone erected to update the story. It declares that Severn was 'the devoted friend and deathbed companion of JOHN KEATS' who was now numbered 'among the immortal poets of England'. For by then Keats's most cherished ambition was on the way to being fulfilled, and his forlorn epitaph refuted. The grave is now a site of pilgrimage for poetry lovers the world over. Scraps of dew-damp paper scrawled with messages of devotion litter the plot, and inscribe and re-inscribe a very different epitaph. So many visitors come in fact, that those who tend the cemetery find it difficult to keep anything green or growing round the grave. A fitting irony. For Keats's final consolation was the beauty of the spot where he would be buried, and that spring flowers would shortly be growing over his anonymous and soon to be forgotten grave.

Spring

Little is reliably known about Keats's early years, and not much about his ancestry. His father Thomas was an ostler (stable-keeper) by profession, but an ambitious one. In October 1794 he married his boss's daughter, Frances Jennings, whose father kept the Swan and Hoop coaching inn and livery stables where Thomas worked. The inn was large and thriving, and stood on what is now the north-west corner of Moorgate and London Wall, just inside the City of London. Keats was born nearby on 31st October 1795. He was followed by George in 1797, and Tom two years later. In 1802 another brother Edward was born, but died within a year, and in 1803 Keats's only sister Fanny joined a growing family that was also rising in the world.

In 1802 Frances's father retired, and the young couple took over the management of the prosperous Swan and Hoop business, and it is probably then that the family came to live there. It is reported that Thomas and Frances even contemplated sending their boys to Harrow, the famous private school. Yet, despite their rising prospects, Harrow was still beyond their means. So in 1803 Keats and his brother George were sent to the same school as their father, in Enfield to the north of London. This choice had a definitive influence on the course of Keats's life, as did an event that happened shortly afterwards.

In the early morning of 15th April 1804 Thomas Keats was nearing home from visiting his sons in Enfield, when he was thrown from his horse on the City Road. His skull was fractured, and he died later that day. With this fatal tumble, the family's prospects tumbled too. Keats's mother marries a man called William Rawlings two months later, and they take over the management of the Swan and Hoop. The marriage isn't a success, and before long Frances consigns her young family to the care of her parents, and disappears from their lives. In 1805 Frances's own father dies, and disputes over his will ensue. These complications meant that Keats would never know about or gain access to his full inheritance. It remained obscured in the dark deliberations of the Court of Chancery, which, as any reader of Dickens's *Bleak House* knows, is to abandon all hope.

In 1809, when Keats was thirteen, his mother returned. The children were living with their grandmother at Church Street, Edmonton, not far from the boys' school in Enfield. Her return appears to have had a profound and lasting effect on her eldest son. For it is then that Keats displayed his passion for literature for the very first time. This, as a schoolfellow recalls, 'came out rather suddenly and unexpectedly'. For Keats, as a child, was 'not attached to books', but to fighting:

> He would fight any one – morning, noon, and night; his brothers among the rest... [But he was] *not* Literary – *his love of books and poetry manifested itself chiefly about a year before he left school.* In all active exercises – he excelled. The generosity and daring of his character with the extreme beauty & animation of his face made I remember an impression on me... This violence & vehemence – this pugnacity & generosity of disposition – in passions of tears or outrageous fits of laughter – always in extremes – will help to paint Keats in his boyhood.

Keats, by his own admission, remained a creature of passion all his life, claiming in July 1818 how he carried 'all matters to an extreme – so that when I have a little vexation it grows in five

Minutes into a theme for Sophocles'. And he never lost what another schoolfellow termed his 'terrier courage'. For we hear how in 1819, the published poet, feted by a literary circle, was found brawling in the streets of north London with a butcher's boy who had been tormenting a kitten. Keats won the contest, despite being just over five foot tall fully grown, and his opponent (as befits a bullying butcher's boy) something of a bruiser. Such accounts identify an abiding aspect of Keats's character, and help to correct the once prevalent picture of the wilting weakling destroyed by hostile reviews.

Keats was no weakling. And we can see clearly the same courage, conviction, and fiery independence, whether he is hurling himself against a bully, or into the world of literature he discovered in his final year at school, and which became his ruling passion thereafter. From being indifferent to learning, he became insatiable. Charles Cowden Clarke, the headmaster's son and Keats's great friend and earliest mentor, recalls how 'He was at work before the first school-hour began, and that was at seven o'clock; and almost all the intervening times of recreation were so devoted... He must in those last months have exhausted the school library.' Keats was on a mission to make up for lost time, and was soon carrying off all the prizes for academic achievement.

At first he appears to have read widely and indiscriminately; then, as Clarke recalls, 'his constantly recurrent sources of attraction were Tooke's *Pantheon*, Lemprière's *Classical Dictionary* which he appeared to *learn*, and Spence's *Polymetus.*' In such works Keats 'acquired his perfect intimacy with the Greek mythology', which his poetic imagination would haunt incessantly. This vanished world no doubt offered a welcome refuge from reality, and the tragic circumstances that overshadowed his mother's welcome return. For when Frances reappeared in 1809, she was already gravely ill.

As Keats grew rapidly in learning, so his mother declined in health, steadily succumbing to the consumption (what we now call tuberculosis) that would eventually claim all of her sons. Devoted to his mother, Keats took on the responsibility of nursing her when he was home from school, feeding her, administering her medicine, reading to her, and jealously guarding his last few months with a mother who had been absent for half his life. When she died in March 1810 he was devastated, withdrawing into himself, and then deeper still into the world of literature. This world he continued to explore with unabated hunger – even when his formal schooling ended that summer, and he started his apprenticeship as an apothecary.

Keats's great passion was literature; but there was no question that this fourteen-year-old orphan, whose inheritance was ensnared in legal deliberation, could at this point pursue anything but a practical path in life. And so he commenced his training under Thomas Hammond of Church Street, Edmonton, not far from his grandmother and siblings. Keats may have believed medicine was his calling while nursing his mother, and he appears to have taken to it well. Clarke, who remained Keats's closest friend during this period, recalled that 'this was the most placid period of his painful life.' It was also a time of great changes in the profession. In 1815, the very year he was due to end his training, an Act was passed requiring a further year's surgical study at a teaching hospital, to qualify to be what is now the equivalent of a general practitioner. Keats enrolled at Guy's Hospital in the Borough, just by London Bridge, that autumn and settled down to the duties and pleasures of the life of a student in London. Some early lines scrawled on the cover of a fellow student's lecture notebook suggest the latter claimed a good deal of his youthful attention.

Give Me Women, Wine and Snuff

Give me women, wine and snuff
Until I cry out 'hold, enough!'

You may do so sans objection
Till the day of resurrection;
For bless my beard they aye shall be
My beloved Trinity.

Although Keats would later abandon medicine for poetry, the sensibility and knowledge instilled in him through his seven years' training never entirely left him. A decided floral fixation in his verse may have been partly fostered by the botanical lore central to his profession. The sure eye that once read the body for eloquent signs of illness, would later paint a palpable world with vivid actuality. While an awareness of suffering, gained both professionally and personally, often intrudes upon and over-shadows a poetry that displays both the human skin in warm sensual abundance and the skull beneath it too.

Keats's literary education ran apace with his medical training during these years, and took up most of his leisure time. In this Clarke, seven years his senior, continued to play a formative role. Although Clarke, looking back in 1861, would claim that Keats 'was a true poet, too – a poet "born, not manufactured", a poet in grain', we might fairly see Clarke himself as 'midwife' in this process, something Keats acknowledges in a poem 'To Charles Cowden Clarke' (from September 1816).

from To Charles Cowden Clarke

Thus have I thought; and days on days have flown
Slowly, or rapidly – unwilling still
For you to try my dull, unlearned quill.
Nor should I now, but that I've known you long;
That you first taught me all the sweets of song:
The grand, the sweet, the terse, the free, the fine;
What swell'd with pathos, and what right divine:

Spenserian vowels that elope with ease,
And float along like birds o'er summer seas;
Miltonian storms, and more, Miltonian tenderness;
Michael in arms, and more, meek Eve's fair slenderness.
Who read for me the sonnet swelling loudly
Up to its climax and then dying proudly?
Who found for me the grandeur of the ode,
Growing, like Atlas, stronger from its load?
Who let me taste that more than cordial dram,
The sharp, the rapier-pointed epigram?
Show'd me that epic was of all the king,
Round, vast, and spanning all like Saturn's ring?
You too upheld the veil from Clio's beauty,
And pointed out the patriot's stern duty;
The might of Alfred, and the shaft of Tell;
The hand of Brutus, that so grandly fell
Upon a tyrant's head. Ah! had I never seen,
Or known your kindness, what might I have been?
What my enjoyments in my youthful years,
Bereft of all that now my life endears?
And can I e'er these benefits forget?
And can I e'er repay the friendly debt?
No, doubly no; – yet should these rhymings please,
I shall roll on the grass with two-fold ease:
For I have long time been my fancy feeding
With hopes that you would one day think the reading
Of my rough verses not an hour misspent;
Should it e'er be so, what a rich content!

During his apprenticeship in Edmonton Keats would regularly visit Clarke in Enfield, and they would spend the whole time reading or discussing poetry. On one occasion it was Spenser's *Faerie Queene*. As Clarke recalls, Keats 'went through it as a young horse would through a spring meadow – ramping'.

Ramping and evidently absorbing; for the Elizabethan poet would prove a major influence on Keats, whose first known poem written the following year (1814), is an 'Imitation of Spenser'.

Imitation of Spenser

Now Morning from her orient chamber came,
And her first footsteps touch'd a verdant hill;
Crowning its lawny crest with amber flame,
Silv'ring the untainted gushes of its rill;
Which, pure from mossy beds, did down distill,
And after parting beds of simple flowers,
By many streams a little lake did fill,
Which round its marge reflected woven bowers,
And, in its middle space, a sky that never lowers.

There the king-fisher saw his plumage bright
Vieing with fish of brilliant dye below;
Whose silken fins, and golden scales' light
Cast upward, through the waves, a ruby glow:
There saw the swan his neck of arched snow,
And oar'd himself along with majesty;
Sparkled his jetty eyes; his feet did show
Beneath the waves like Afric's ebony,
And on his back a fay reclined voluptuously.

Ah! could I tell the wonders of an isle
That in that fairest lake had placed been,
I could e'en Dido of her brief beguile;
Or rob from aged Lear his bitter teen:
For sure so fair a place was never seen,
Of all that ever charm'd romantic eye:
It seem'd an emerald in the silver sheen

> *Of the bright waters; or as when on high,*
> *Through clouds of fleecy white, laughs the cærulean sky.*

> *And all around it dipp'd luxuriously*
> *Slopings of verdure through the glossy tide,*
> *Which, as it were in gentle amity,*
> *Rippled delighted up the flowery side;*
> *As if to glean the ruddy tears, it tried,*
> *Which fell profusely from the rose-tree stem!*
> *Haply it was the workings of its pride,*
> *In strife to throw upon the shore a gem*
> *Outvieing all the buds in Flora's diadem.*

Two years later, when they were both living in London, Clarke borrowed a copy of Homer's *Iliad* and *Odyssey* translated by Shakespeare's contemporary George Chapman. The two friends read it through the night, and, on the two mile walk from Clerkenwell to his lodgings in the Borough, Keats composed a poem commemorating this shared literary discovery. 'On First Looking in to Chapman's Homer', which Keats penned immediately on reaching home, is undoubtedly his first truly assured poetic performance.

On First Looking into Chapman's Homer

> *Much have I travell'd in the realms of gold,*
> *And many goodly states and kingdoms seen;*
> *Round many western islands have I been*
> *Which bards in fealty to Apollo hold.*
> *Oft of one wide expanse had I been told*
> *That deep-brow'd Homer rules as his demesne;*
> *Yet did I never breathe its pure serene*
> *Till I heard Chapman speak out loud and bold:*

Then felt I like some watcher of the skies
*   When a new planet swims into his ken;*
Or like stout Cortez when with eagle eyes
*   He star'd at the Pacific – and all his men*
Look'd at each other with a wild surmise –
Silent, upon a peak in Darien.

By the time Keats wrote this poem (October 1816) it must have been evident where his true interests and aspirations lay. In May of that year his first poem, 'O Solitude', had been published in Leigh Hunt's *The Examiner*.

O Solitude! if I must with thee dwell

O Solitude! if I must with thee dwell,
*   Let it not be among the jumbled heap*
*   Of murky buildings; climb with me the steep, –*
Nature's observatory – whence the dell,
Its flowery slopes, its river's crystal swell,
*   May seem a span; let me thy vigils keep*
*   'Mongst boughs pavillion'd, where the deer's swift leap*
Startles the wild bee from the fox-glove bell.
But though I'll gladly trace these scenes with thee,
*   Yet the sweet converse of an innocent mind,*
*   Whose words are images of thoughts refin'd,*
Is my soul's pleasure; and it sure must be
*   Almost the highest bliss of human-kind,*
When to thy haunts two kindred spirits flee.

This was followed by 'Chapman's Homer' in December 1816 in the same journal. Despite passing his examinations quite respectably, rising through the ranks to become a 'dresser' (assisting the demonstrating surgeon), and prudently acquiring his licence to practise as an apothecary, his heart was clearly elsewhere. As he confided to Clarke towards the end of his training, 'The other day, for instance, during the lecture, there came a sunbeam into the room, and with it a whole troop of creatures floating in the ray; and I was off with them to Oberon and Fairy-land.' Such dreamy distractions were hardly conducive to the practice of surgery. Keats had to throw himself body and soul into his true vocation, and so shortly after his twenty-first birthday he officially resolved to abandon the career upon which he had invested nearly all of his known inheritance. This was a brave thing to do, and we see again his plucky independence of spirit asserting itself. Poetry was for those with means, leisure and connections. Byron may have woken up to find himself famous (and a best-seller), with the publication of the first two cantos of his poem *Childe Harold* in March 1812; but Byron was a lord, had attended a major private school and Cambridge University, and had already travelled through many of the lands of Classical antiquity that Keats could only dream about in verse. So when Keats went to inform Richard Abbey (a tea-dealer who had been the Keats's guardian since 1814) of his decision, the older man's response was 'not moderate'. Declaring:

John, you are either Mad or a Fool, to talk in so absurd a Manner. My Mind is made up, said the younger very quietly. I know that I possess Abilities greater than most Men, and therefore I am determined to gain my Living by exercising them.

We can now see that Keats was right in his estimation of his abilities, and we can be thankful he formed this brave determination. But we can also see that Abbey, a practical man of business, had a point. Abilities, even the towering, unique genius that we can now recognise residing in this spirited and ambitious young man, are no guarantee of success, or at least not in its proper season.

Keats was idealistic and ambitious, but he was not quite the 'silly Boy' Abbey had called him when he prophesied the 'speedy Termination to his inconsiderate Enterprise'. He knew he had talent, but also that he had a lot of work to do if he was to fulfil his potential.

Keats had been writing poems for only two years, and avidly consuming them for six. As 'On First Reading Chapman's Homer' suggests, discovery-inspiration-composition formed a closely knit chain which he forged in verse. Before Keats could be among the greats, he first had to master them. No primrose path of dilettante dalliance this, poetry had replaced medicine as a demanding full-time discipline. 'Sleep and Poetry' (October–December 1816) sets this new course out clearly:

from Sleep and Poetry

Stop and consider! life is but a day;
A fragile dew-drop on its perilous way
From a tree's summit; a poor Indian's sleep
While his boat hastens to the monstrous steep
Of Montmorenci. Why so sad a moan?
Life is the rose's hope while yet unblown;
The reading of an ever-changing tale;
The light uplifting of a maiden's veil;
A pigeon tumbling in clear summer air;
A laughing school-boy, without grief or care,
Riding the springy branches of an elm.

O for ten years, that I may overwhelm
Myself in poesy; so I may do the deed
That my own soul has to itself decreed.
Then will I pass the countries that I see

In long perspective, and continually
Taste their pure fountains. First the realm I'll pass
Of Flora, and old Pan: sleep in the grass,
Feed upon apples red, and strawberries,
And choose each pleasure that my fancy sees;
Catch the white-handed nymphs in shady places,
To woo sweet kisses from averted faces, –
Play with their fingers, touch their shoulders white
Into a pretty shrinking with a bite
As hard as lips can make it: till agreed,
A lovely tale of human life we'll read.
And one will teach a tame dove how it best
May fan the cool air gently o'er my rest;
Another, bending o'er her nimble tread,
Will set a green robe floating round her head,
And still will dance with ever varied ease,
Smiling upon the flowers and the trees:
Another will entice me on, and on
Through almond blossoms and rich cinnamon;
Till in the bosom of a leafy world
We rest in silence, like two gems upcurl'd
In the recesses of a pearly shell.

While poetry provided inspiration, certain individuals offered something more immediately valuable in his transition from apprentice to published poet – encouragement. The most important of these was Leigh Hunt. Charles Cowden Clarke lists Hunt's journal, *The Examiner*, as one of the staples of Keats's reading in the library at Enfield, and its radical agenda was in keeping with the school's liberal sympathies. Clarke knew Hunt, and when he introduced Keats to him in October 1816, he was effectively transferring his mentor's mantle to this notorious poet, journalist and political firebrand. Hunt had recently been released from a two-year prison sentence for supposedly libelling the Prince Regent. Keats commemorated the event with a sonnet brimming with righteous political fervour, and he obviously admired the man to whom he entrusted the publication of his first lines in print, and to whom he would dedicate his first published volume of verse.

It was, according to Clarke, 'a red-letter day in the young poet's life' when he accompanied him to the Vale of Health below Hampstead Heath, to meet his idol and editor. Hunt reciprocated with admiration for Keats, which he made public in *The Examiner* in December 1816. Here he announced Keats as one of three rising stars of poetry (alongside John Hamilton Reynolds and Percy Bysshe Shelley). He quoted 'On First Looking into Chapman's Homer' in full, and spoke of other gems he had seen in manuscript. Hunt's very public patronage, earning Keats's equally public gratitude, was invaluable in launching him into the world of letters and giving him the confidence to pursue his dreams. Yet it also served to identify him closely with the radical Hunt, giving his Tory opponents another whipping boy for their enmities in due course.

Through Clarke, then Hunt, Keats swiftly became part of a loose circle of poets, artists and men of letters, and enjoyed the fellowship of like-minded individuals who recognised his talents, publicised his promise and encouraged his soaring ambitions. This included Charles and James Ollier, who agreed to publish his first volume of verse. This slim volume of *Poems* by John Keats appeared in March 1817, bearing an engraving of Shakespeare, an epigraph from Spenser and a dedication to Hunt. It also carried the highest expectations of Keats's friends, who according to Clarke 'expected that it would create a sensation in the literary world'. But as Clarke lamented, 'Alas! it might have emerged in Timbuctoo with stronger chance of fame and favor.' It sold badly, and poet and publisher parted ways acrimoniously. But, as Keats would learn the next time he ventured into print, there are possibly worse fates than indifference for a rising poet to endure.

Not everyone around Keats was so enthusiastic about this first published volume. Shelley, who was never a close friend of Keats, had attempted to dissuade him from publication. His criticism was no doubt constructive, yet Keats was always wary of the aristocratic rebel, whom he met through Hunt, and who soon eclipsed him as the latter's principal protégé. Shelley thought it premature, and so it is. It comprises mostly 'occasional' verse about people the public or literary establishment either didn't know (like the unknown poet's family), or might not much care for (such as its radical dedicatory, Hunt). Its more ambitious pieces, such as 'Sleep and Poetry' or 'I Stood Tip-Toe up on a Little Hill' exhibit a certain breathy luxuriance as Keats tried hard, a bit too hard, to emulate the poets he loved. Yet we might discern even here anticipations of a style and voice that, once controlled and polished by his own mature discernment, would emerge into what we recognise as quintessentially Keatsian. Extravagance would in time blossom into full sensual richness, and emulation would nurture an assured and distinctive genius.

Summer

Keats developed quickly. Indeed his growth as a poet, from apprenticeship to immortality, is perhaps the most rapid and spectacular in English letters. By the time this first volume appeared he was already preparing to express himself on a more ambitious canvas. In spring 1817 he threw down the gauntlet to his own ability, asking, 'Did our great Poets ever write short Pieces?' Well, yes they did. Spenser, Sidney, Shakespeare, Milton, Dante, all wrote sonnets and odes as well as the longer pieces for which they are principally known. Milton was fifty when he started *Paradise Lost*, exactly double the length of Keats's full lifespan. Keats's rather premature insistence on mastering longer forms is a measure of his urgent desire to stand alongside the immortals he idolised, and remained a constant goad to his ambition throughout his creative years.

In spring 1817 Keats began *Endymion*, his first attempt to write a long poem. The poetic apprentice who had asked for ten years to 'overwhelm' himself in poetry, may have seen this as part of his 'qualification' as a poet. On starting the poem he referred to it as a 'test, a trial of my Powers of Imagination and chiefly of my Invention... by which I must make 4000 Lines of one bare circumstance and fill them with Poetry...' 'Test', 'trial', 'must'? Having replaced one formal course of study with another, Keats embarked on his voyage to greatness in a highly disciplined way.

He also began journeying in the literal sense too. In mid March 1817 he set off to the Isle of Wight to start his poem, initiating a pattern of restlessness that would culminate in his desperate trip to Italy three and a half years later. We might view this as the lot of the orphan, who had hardly known a settled home life. But he also travelled with a purpose: to absorb fresh scenes and influences. Hampstead was a fine and leafy place, and must have seemed like Arcadia after the mists and mire of Moorgate or the dirt and din of the Borough. Yet if Keats was to scale Parnassus, he must stand tip-toe on some more varied and demanding terrains than the little hills of north London. This bore fruit in his sonnet, 'On the Sea', written in mid April in the Isle of Wight.

> It keeps eternal whisperings around
>   Desolate shores, and with its mighty swell
>   Gluts twice ten thousand Caverns, till the spell
> Of Hecate leaves them their old shadowy sound.
> Often 'tis in such gentle temper found,
>   That scarcely will the very smallest shell
>   Be mov'd for days from where it sometime fell,
> When last the winds of Heaven were unbound.
> Oh ye! who have your eye-balls vex'd and tir'd,
>   Feast them upon the wideness of the Sea;
>   Oh ye! whose ears are dinn'd with uproar rude,
>   Or fed too much with cloying melody –
>   Sit ye near some old Cavern's Mouth, and brood
> Until ye start, as if the sea-nymphs quir'd!

Keats also travelled to find an environment more conducive to study and creativity. He had been living with his brothers first on Cheapside, and more recently at Well Walk in his beloved Hampstead. He was gregarious and fun-loving, a side rarely seen in the canonical poems, but which comes out strongly in his letters (where puns, jokes, ditties and bawdy jostle with his serious verse or aesthetic theories). He was rarely alone, and Keats the young man, loyal friend and caring brother, generally preferred it that way. But Keats the poet on a mission to greatness had to resist such temptations, and discipline himself into solitary productivity. So he packed his bag with books – a collected Shakespeare uppermost – and set off by coach to Southampton, travelling on the outside, as was his practice, to save money.

Endymion is Keats's attempt to write a classical verse romance in the style of Shakespeare's *Venus and Adonis*. And like that poem, it uses a myth of a love between a deity and a mortal as an extended exercise in poetic description, embellishment and incident. Keats had touched on this story in his poem 'I Stood Tip-Toe up on a Little Hill', as an allegory of the poet's (often forlorn) desire for the ideal.

from I stood tip-toe upon a little hill

Where had he been, from whose warm head out-flew
That sweetest of all songs, that ever new,
That aye refreshing pure deliciousness,
Coming ever to bless
The wanderer by moonlight? to him bringing
Shapes from the invisible world, unearthly singing
From out the middle air, from flowery nests,
And from the pillowy silkiness that rests
Full in the speculation of the stars.
Ah! surely he had burst our mortal bars;
Into some wond'rous region he had gone,
To search for thee, divine Endymion!

He was a Poet, sure a lover too,
Who stood on Latmus' top, what time there blew
Soft breezes from the myrtle vale below;

And brought in faintness solemn, sweet, and slow
A hymn from Dian's temple; while upswelling,
The incense went to her own starry dwelling.
But though her face was clear as infant's eyes,
Though she stood smiling o'er the sacrifice,
The Poet wept at her so piteous fate,
Wept that such beauty should be desolate:
So in fine wrath some golden sounds he won,
And gave meek Cynthia her Endymion.

Queen of the wide air; thou most lovely queen
Of all the brightness that mine eyes have seen!
As thou exceedest all things in thy shine,
So every tale, does this sweet tale of thine.
O for three words of honey, that I might
Tell but one wonder of thy bridal night!

Keats expands on this idea over his proposed 4,000 lines, exploring such concerns as beauty, dreaming versus reality and poetic creation, which would become the staples of his art. It opens with some of Keats's most famous lines:

from Endymion: A Poetic Romance

A thing of beauty is a joy for ever:
Its loveliness increases; it will never
Pass into nothingness; but still will keep
A bower quiet for us, and a sleep
Full of sweet dreams, and health, and quiet breathing.
Therefore, on every morrow, are we wreathing
A flowery band to bind us to the earth,
Spite of despondence, of the inhuman dearth

Of noble natures, of the gloomy days,
Of all the unhealthy and o'er-darkened ways
Made for our searching: yes, in spite of all,
Some shape of beauty moves away the pall
From our dark spirits. Such the sun, the moon,
Trees old, and young, sprouting a shady boon
For simple sheep; and such are daffodils
With the green world they live in; and clear rills
That for themselves a cooling covert make
'Gainst the hot season; the mid forest brake,
Rich with a sprinkling of fair musk-rose blooms:
And such too is the grandeur of the dooms
We have imagined for the mighty dead;
All lovely tales that we have heard or read:
An endless fountain of immortal drink,
Pouring unto us from the heaven's brink.

   Nor do we merely feel these essences
For one short hour; no, even as the trees
That whisper round a temple become soon
Dear as the temple's self, so does the moon,
The passion poesy, glories infinite,
Haunt us till they become a cheering light
Unto our souls, and bound to us so fast,
That, whether there be shine, or gloom o'ercast,
They always must be with us, or we die.

   Therefore, 'tis with full happiness that I
Will trace the story of Endymion.
The very music of the name has gone
Into my being, and each pleasant scene
Is growing fresh before me as the green
Of our own vallies: so I will begin
Now while I cannot hear the city's din;
Now while the early budders are just new,

And run in mazes of the youngest hue
About old forests; while the willow trails
Its delicate amber; and the dairy pails
Bring home increase of milk. And, as the year
Grows lush in juicy stalks, I'll smoothly steer
My little boat, for many quiet hours,
With streams that deepen freshly into bowers.
Many and many a verse I hope to write,
Before the daisies, vermeil rimm'd and white,
Hide in deep herbage; and ere yet the bees
Hum about the globes of clover and sweet peas,
I must be near the middle of my story.
O may no wintry season, bare and hoary,
See it half finish'd: but let Autumn bold,
With universal tinge of sober gold,
Be all about me when I make an end.
And now at once, adventuresome, I send
My herald thought into a wilderness:
There let its trumpet blow, and quickly dress
My uncertain path with green, that I may speed
Easily onward, thorough flowers and weed.

The introductory stanza self-consciously outlines the poetic task and its timeframe, and reveals Keats as a strict taskmaster to his own ambition. But then he had to be. Although he saw *Endymion* as a poetic rite of passage, a feat of endurance to prove his invention, he also hoped it would bring more success and sales than his first volume. Keats's obsession with long poems had other motivations than the purely artistic. It was his long verse narrative, published in parts, that made Lord Byron rich as well as famous immediately on publication; and if Keats was serious about living by his pen he had to keep a keen eye on the market. Besides, his new publisher Taylor and Hessey lent him £20 in anticipation of the sales from his poem, so the sooner he completed his poem the sooner they could all recoup their investments. Alone for the first time, a full-time, professional poet for the first time, he had to approach the task professionally.

Yet Keats found the sustained writing demanded by his trial irksome. He was alone with himself, and what he termed that May 'a horrid Morbidity of Temperament', which he feared might prove to be the 'greatest Enemy and stumbling block' to his poetic plans. Perhaps solitude wasn't so conducive to creation after all. He became restless, disenchanted with the Isle of Wight, and looked to move on. By the beginning of May he was at the seaside resort Margate with his brother Tom, who was starting to show signs of the consumption that would cut his life even shorter than the poet's. Sea air and water were prescribed for all manner of complaints at the time, and Keats didn't need much encouragement to end his solitary literary vigil to look after his frail younger brother. From Margate he travelled to Canterbury, then on to near Hastings; but by June he was back in Hampstead, not even half-way through his poem.

The 'Hymn to Pan'
from Endymion Book I

…Thus ending, on the shrine he heap'd a spire
Of teeming sweets, enkindling sacred fire;
Anon he stain'd the thick and spongy sod
With wine, in honour of the shepherd-god.
Now while the earth was drinking it, and while
Bay leaves were crackling in the fragrant pile,
And gummy frankincense was sparkling bright
'Neath smothering parsley, and a hazy light
Spread greyly eastward, thus a chorus sang:

'Oh thou, whose mighty palace roof doth hang
From jagged trunks, and overshadoweth

Eternal whispers, glooms, the birth, life, death
Of unseen flowers in heavy peacefulness;
Who lov'st to see the hamadryads dress
Their ruffled locks where meeting hazels darken;
And through whole solemn hours dost sit, and hearken
The dreary melody of bedded reeds –
In desolate places, where dank moisture breeds
The pipy hemlock to strange overgrowth;
Bethinking thee, how melancholy loth
Thou wast to lose fair Syrinx – do thou now,
By thy love's milky brow!
By all the trembling mazes that she ran,
Hear us, great Pan!

   'O thou, for whose soul-soothing quiet, turtles
Passion their voices cooingly 'mong myrtles,
What time thou wanderest at eventide
Through sunny meadows, that outskirt the side
Of thine enmossed realms: O thou, to whom
Broad leaved fig trees even now foredoom
Their ripen'd fruitage; yellow girted bees
Their golden honeycombs; our village leas
Their fairest blossom'd beans and poppied corn;
The chuckling linnet its five young unborn,
To sing for thee; low creeping strawberries
Their summer coolness; pent up butterflies
Their freckled wings; yea, the fresh budding year
All its completions – be quickly near,
By every wind that nods the mountain pine,
O forester divine!

   'Thou, to whom every faun and satyr flies
For willing service; whether to surprise
The squatted hare while in half sleeping fit;
Or upward ragged precipices flit

To save poor lambkins from the eagle's maw;
Or by mysterious enticement draw
Bewildered shepherds to their path again;
Or to tread breathless round the frothy main,
And gather up all fancifullest shells
For thee to tumble into Naiads' cells,
And, being hidden, laugh at their out-peeping;
Or to delight thee with fantastic leaping,
The while they pelt each other on the crown
With silvery oak apples, and fir cones brown –
By all the echoes that about thee ring,
Hear us, O satyr king!

    'O Hearkener to the loud clapping shears
While ever and anon to his shorn peers
A ram goes bleating: Winder of the horn,
When snouted wild-boars routing tender corn
Anger our huntsmen: Breather round our farms,
To keep off mildews, and all weather harms:
Strange ministrant of undescribed sounds,
That come a swooning over hollow grounds,
And wither drearily on barren moors:
Dread opener of the mysterious doors
Leading to universal knowledge – see,
Great son of Dryope,
The many that are come to pay their vows
With leaves about their brows!

    'Be still the unimaginable lodge
For solitary thinkings; such as dodge
Conception to the very bourne of heaven,
Then leave the naked brain: be still the leaven,
That spreading in this dull and clodded earth
Gives it a touch ethereal – a new birth:
Be still a symbol of immensity;

A firmament reflected in a sea;
An element filling the space between;
An unknown – but no more: we humbly screen
With uplift hands our foreheads, lowly bending,
And giving out a shout most heaven rending,
Conjure thee to receive our humble Paean,
Upon thy Mount Lycean!'

Keats also visited Oxford at the end of the summer, spending over a month with a relatively new friend, Benjamin Bailey. Bailey was a student at Magdalen Hall, reading for holy orders, and the cloistral hush combined with a convivial and studious company proved conducive for the restless, distracted poet. Bailey would later recall a different Keats from the indolent 'morbid' procrastinator of the early summer. 'He wrote, & I read, sometimes at the same table... He sat down to his task, – which was about 50 lines a day... and wrote with as much regularity, & apparently as much ease, as he wrote his letters...' They did, however, find time to visit Stratford-upon-Avon, Shakespeare's birthplace, and so for Keats the holiest of holies.

By November *Endymion* was finished, and his 4,000 line trial complete. Yet, it fell short of his expectations and standards. He had outgrown its conception even as he realised it, and could see mostly its imperfections. In September, before he had even finished the third book he was telling his friend, the painter Benjamin Robert Haydon, 'My Ideas with respect to it I assure you are very low – and I would write the subject thoroughly again.' Keats was often his own most exacting critic, with his ambition and intellectual development ever outpacing and upbraiding his achievements. These inner conflicts he would sometimes make public, as with the misguided preface he insisted on publishing for *Endymion*. This drew the reader's attention to the 'great inexperience, immaturity, and every error' of the poem, arguably strangling it at birth. What critical response could he have expected for a poem so introduced?

The candidate appears to have failed his self-imposed test. The circumstances are ultimately neither singular nor 'bare' – draped rather, if not smothered, in his decorative extravagances, and distracted by too many picturesque Ovidian set pieces. To be fair, it is far more convincing than the scattered fragments of promise published hitherto. It displays a firmer intellectual grasp, and there are moments of real beauty and more fluent descriptive power; yet Keats has difficulty sustaining this over the course, and making the parts cohere into a whole. It shows his comparative youth, and that his poetic vision was still work in progress.

from Endymion
Book II

> ... *After a thousand mazes overgone,*
> *At last, with sudden step, he came upon*
> *A chamber, myrtle wall'd, embowered high,*
> *Full of light, incense, tender minstrelsy,*
> *And more of beautiful and strange beside:*
> *For on a silken couch of rosy pride,*
> *In midst of all, there lay a sleeping youth*
> *Of fondest beauty; fonder, in fair sooth,*
> *Than sighs could fathom, or contentment reach:*
> *And coverlids gold-tinted like the peach,*
> *Or ripe October's faded marigolds,*
> *Fell sleek about him in a thousand folds –*
> *Not hiding up an Apollonian curve*
> *Of neck and shoulder, nor the tenting swerve*
> *Of knee from knee, nor ankles pointing light;*
> *But rather, giving them to the filled sight*
> *Officiously. Sideway his face repos'd*

On one white arm, and tenderly unclos'd,
By tenderest pressure, a faint damask mouth
To slumbery pout; just as the morning south
Disparts a dew-lipp'd rose. Above his head,
Four lilly stalks did their white honours wed
To make a coronal; and round him grew
All tendrils green, of every bloom and hue,
Together intertwin'd and trammel'd fresh:
The vine of glossy sprout; the ivy mesh,
Shading its Ethiop berries; and woodbine,
Of velvet leaves and bugle-blooms divine;
Convolvulus in streaked vases flush;
The creeper, mellowing for an autumn blush;
And virgin's bower, trailing airily;
With others of the sisterhood. Hard by,
Stood serene Cupids watching silently.
One, kneeling to a lyre, touch'd the strings,
Muffling to death the pathos with his wings;
And, ever and anon, uprose to look
At the youth's slumber; while another took
A willow-bough, distilling odorous dew,
And shook it on his hair; another flew
In through the woven roof, and fluttering-wise
Rain'd violets upon his sleeping eyes.

   At these enchantments, and yet many more,
The breathless Latmian wonder'd o'er and o'er;
Until, impatient in embarrassment,
He forthright pass'd, and lightly treading went
To that same feather'd lyrist, who straightway,
Smiling, thus whisper'd: 'Though from upper day
Thou art a wanderer, and thy presence here
Might seem unholy, be of happy cheer!
For 'tis the nicest touch of human honour,
When some ethereal and high-favouring donor

Presents immortal bowers to mortal sense;
As now 'tis done to thee, Endymion. Hence
Was I in no wise startled. So recline
Upon these living flowers. Here is wine,
Alive with sparkles – never, I aver,
Since Ariadne was a vintager,
So cool a purple: taste these juicy pears,
Sent me by sad Vertumnus, when his fears
Were high about Pomona: here is cream,
Deepening to richness from a snowy gleam;
Sweeter than that nurse Amalthea skimm'd
For the boy Jupiter: and here, undimm'd
By any touch, a bunch of blooming plums
Ready to melt between an infant's gums:
And here is manna pick'd from Syrian trees,
In starlight, by the three Hesperides.
Feast on, and meanwhile I will let thee know
Of all these things around us.' He did so,
Still brooding o'er the cadence of his lyre;
And thus: 'I need not any hearing tire
By telling how the sea-born goddess pin'd
For a mortal youth, and she strove to bind
Him all in all unto her doting self.
Who would not be so prison'd? but, fond elf,
He was content to let her amorous plea
Faint through his careless arms; content to see
An unseiz'd heaven dying at his feet;
Content, O fool! to make a cold retreat,
When on the pleasant grass such love, lovelorn,
Lay sorrowing; when every tear was born
Of diverse passion; when her lips and eyes
Were clos'd in sullen moisture, and quick sighs
Came vex'd and pettish through her nostrils small.
Hush! no exclaim – yet, justly mightst thou call
Curses upon his head. – I was half glad,

But my poor mistress went distract and mad,
When the boar tusk'd him: so away she flew
To Jove's high throne, and by her plainings drew
Immortal tear-drops down the thunderer's beard;
Whereon it was decreed he should be rear'd
Each summer time to life. Lo! this is he,
That same Adonis, safe in the privacy
Of this still region all his winter-sleep.
Aye, sleep; for when our love-sick queen did weep
Over his waned corse, the tremulous shower
Heal'd up the wound, and, with a balmy power,
Medicined death to a lengthened drowsiness:
The which she fills with visions, and doth dress
In all this quiet luxury; and hath set
Us young immortals, without any let,
To watch his slumber through. 'Tis well nigh pass'd,
Even to a moment's filling up, and fast
She scuds with summer breezes, to pant through
The first long kiss, warm firstling, to renew
Embower'd sports in Cytherea's isle.
Look! how those winged listeners all this while
Stand anxious: see! behold!' This clamant word
Broke through the careful silence; for they heard
A rustling noise of leaves, and out there flutter'd
Pigeons and doves: Adonis something mutter'd,
The while one hand, that erst upon his thigh
Lay dormant, mov'd convuls'd and gradually
Up to his forehead. Then there was a hum
Of sudden voices, echoing, 'Come! come!
Arise! awake! Clear summer has forth walk'd
Unto the clover-sward, and she has talk'd
Full soothingly to every nested finch:
Rise, Cupids! or we'll give the blue-bell pinch
To your dimpled arms. Once more sweet life begin!'
At this, from every side they hurried in

Rubbing their sleepy eyes with lazy wrists,
And doubling overhead their little fists
In backward yawns. But all were soon alive:
For as delicious wine doth, sparkling, dive
In nectar'd clouds and curls through water fair,
So from the arbour roof down swell'd an air
Odorous and enlivening; making all
To laugh, and play, and sing, and loudly call
For their sweet queen: when lo! the wreathed green
Disparted, and far upward could be seen
Blue heaven, and a silver car, air-borne,
Whose silent wheels, fresh wet from clouds of morn,
Spun off a drizzling dew, – which falling chill
On soft Adonis' shoulders, made him still
Nestle and turn uneasily about.
Soon were the white doves plain, with neck stretch'd out,
And silken traces lighten'd in descent;
And soon, returning from love's banishment,
Queen Venus leaning downward open arm'd:
Her shadow fell upon his breast, and charm'd
A tumult to his heart, and a new life
Into his eyes. Ah, miserable strife,
But for her comforting! unhappy sight,
But meeting her blue orbs! Who, who can write
Of these first minutes? The unchariest muse
To embracements warm as theirs makes coy excuse.

If Keats was worn out and disconsolate at the end of 1817 there were other causes than the perceived failure of his aesthetic ideals. Winter was approaching, and this presented a fresh trial to Tom's fragile health. Teignmouth in Devon was selected for its milder climate than the damp, foggy capital, and so Tom was dispatched there under the care of George. He was joined by Keats in early March 1818, by which time Tom was spitting blood and clearly wasting away. They had come for better air, but it rained without relent for weeks on end, confining them to their rooms. As Keats complained to John Hamilton Reynolds after over a month of bad weather, 'The Climate here weighs us [down] completely – Tom is quite low spirited. It is impossible to live in a country which is continually under hatches – Who would live in the region of Mists, Game Laws, indemnity Bills, etc. when there is such a place as Italy?' Indeed.

Keats embarked on *Isabella, or The Pot of Basil* while he was at Teignmouth, evoking the blue skies of Florentine Romance, as the relentless rains of the present beat down. Keats adapted the theme from Boccaccio, turning it into a rather macabre tale of desire, devotion and treachery. Characteristically Keats felt its faults most keenly, and rejected the poem as 'too smokeable' (easily ridiculed) as soon as he had completed it. Yet it is arguably his first successfully sustained narrative poem. He sticks to the theme, and sees it through with few deviations. The more regular stanzic structure, which he would employ again with an even surer hand in 'The Eve of St Agnes', focused his thoughts and controlled his expression. Keats was slowly but surely starting to shine.

Isabella;
or,
The Pot of Basil
A Story from Boccaccio

I

Fair Isabel, poor simple Isabel!
    Lorenzo, a young palmer in Love's eye!
They could not in the self-same mansion dwell
    Without some stir of heart, some malady;
They could not sit at meals but feel how well

It soothed each to be the other by;
They could not, sure, beneath the same roof sleep
But to each other dream, and nightly weep.

II

With every morn their love grew tenderer,
  With every eve deeper and tenderer still;
He might not in house, field, or garden stir,
  But her full shape would all his seeing fill;
And his continual voice was pleasanter
  To her, than noise of trees or hidden rill;
Her lute-string gave an echo of his name,
She spoilt her half-done broidery with the same.

III

He knew whose gentle hand was at the latch,
  Before the door had given her to his eyes;
And from her chamber-window he would catch
  Her beauty farther than the falcon spies;
And constant as her vespers would he watch,
  Because her face was turn'd to the same skies;
And with sick longing all the night outwear,
To hear her morning-step upon the stair.

IV

A whole long month of May in this sad plight
  Made their cheeks paler by the break of June:
'To-morrow will I bow to my delight,
  To-morrow will I ask my lady's boon.' –
'O may I never see another night,
  Lorenzo, if thy lips breathe not love's tune.' –
So spake they to their pillows; but, alas,
Honeyless days and days did he let pass;

V

Until sweet Isabella's untouch'd cheek
  Fell sick within the rose's just domain,
Fell thin as a young mother's, who doth seek
  By every lull to cool her infant's pain:
'How ill she is,' said he, 'I may not speak,
  And yet I will, and tell my love all plain:
If looks speak love-laws, I will drink her tears,
And at the least 'twill startle off her cares.'

So said he one fair morning, and all day
  His heart beat awfully against his side;
And to his heart he inwardly did pray
  For power to speak; but still the ruddy tide
Stifled his voice, and puls'd resolve away –
  Fever'd his high conceit of such a bride,
Yet brought him to the meekness of a child:
Alas! when passion is both meek and wild!

VII

So once more he had wak'd and anguished
  A dreary night of love and misery,
If Isabel's quick eye had not been wed
  To every symbol on his forehead high;
She saw it waxing very pale and dead,
  And straight all flush'd; so, lisped tenderly,
'Lorenzo!' – here she ceas'd her timid quest,
But in her tone and look he read the rest.

'O Isabella, I can half perceive
  That I may speak my grief into thine ear;

If thou didst ever anything believe,

Believe how I love thee, believe how near
My soul is to its doom: I would not grieve

Thy hand by unwelcome pressing, would not fear
Thine eyes by gazing; but I cannot live
Another night, and not my passion shrive.

IX

'Love! thou art leading me from wintry cold,

Lady! thou leadest me to summer clime,
And I must taste the blossoms that unfold

In its ripe warmth this gracious morning time.'
So said, his erewhile timid lips grew bold,

And poesied with hers in dewy rhyme:
Great bliss was with them, and great happiness
Grew, like a lusty flower in June's caress.

X

Parting they seem'd to tread upon the air,

Twin roses by the zephyr blown apart
Only to meet again more close, and share

The inward fragrance of each other's heart.
She, to her chamber gone, a ditty fair

Sang, of delicious love and honey'd dart;
He with light steps went up a western hill,
And bade the sun farewell, and joy'd his fill.

XI

All close they met again, before the dusk

Had taken from the stars its pleasant veil,
All close they met, all eves, before the dusk

Had taken from the stars its pleasant veil,
Close in a bower of hyacinth and musk,

Unknown of any, free from whispering tale.
Ah! better had it been for ever so,
Than idle ears should pleasure in their woe.

XII

Were they unhappy then? – It cannot be –
    Too many tears for lovers have been shed,
Too many sighs give we to them in fee,
    Too much of pity after they are dead,
Too many doleful stories do we see,
    Whose matter in bright gold were best be read;
Except in such a page where Theseus' spouse
Over the pathless waves towards him bows.

XIII

But, for the general award of love,
    The little sweet doth kill much bitterness;
Though Dido silent is in under-grove,
    And Isabella's was a great distress,
Though young Lorenzo in warm Indian clove
    Was not embalm'd, this truth is not the less –
Even bees, the little almsmen of spring-bowers,
Know there is richest juice in poison-flowers.

XIV

With her two brothers this fair lady dwelt,
    Enriched from ancestral merchandize,
And for them many a weary hand did swelt
    In torched mines and noisy factories,
And many once proud-quiver'd loins did melt
    In blood from stinging whip; – with hollow eyes
Many all day in dazzling river stood,
To take the rich-ored driftings of the flood.

For them the Ceylon diver held his breath,
   And went all naked to the hungry shark;
For them his ears gush'd blood; for them in death
   The seal on the cold ice with piteous bark
Lay full of darts; for them alone did seethe
   A thousand men in troubles wide and dark:
Half-ignorant, they turn'd an easy wheel,
That set sharp racks at work, to pinch and peel.

Why were they proud? Because their marble founts
   Gush'd with more pride than do a wretch's tears? –
Why were they proud? Because fair orange-mounts
   Were of more soft ascent than lazar stairs? –
Why were they proud? Because red-lin'd accounts
   Were richer than the songs of Grecian years? –
Why were they proud? again we ask aloud,
Why in the name of Glory were they proud?

Yet were these Florentines as self-retired
   In hungry pride and gainful cowardice,
As two close Hebrews in that land inspired,
   Paled in and vineyarded from beggar-spies;
The hawks of ship-mast forests – the untired
   And pannier'd mules for ducats and old lies –
Quick cat's-paws on the generous stray-away, –
Great wits in Spanish, Tuscan, and Malay.

How was it these same ledger-men could spy
   Fair Isabella in her downy nest?

How could they find out in Lorenzo's eye
  A straying from his toil? Hot Egypt's pest
Into their vision covetous and sly!
  How could these money-bags see east and west? –
Yet so they did – and every dealer fair
Must see behind, as doth the hunted hare.

XIX

O eloquent and famed Boccaccio!
  Of thee we now should ask forgiving boon,
And of thy spicy myrtles as they blow,
  And of thy roses amorous of the moon,
And of thy lilies, that do paler grow
  Now they can no more hear thy ghittern's tune,
For venturing syllables that ill beseem
The quiet glooms of such a piteous theme.

XX

Grant thou a pardon here, and then the tale
  Shall move on soberly, as it is meet;
There is no other crime, no mad assail
  To make old prose in modern rhyme more sweet:
But it is done – succeed the verse or fail –
  To honour thee, and thy gone spirit greet;
To stead thee as a verse in English tongue,
An echo of thee in the north-wind sung.

XXI

These brethren having found by many signs
  What love Lorenzo for their sister had,
And how she lov'd him too, each unconfines
  His bitter thoughts to other, well nigh mad
That he, the servant of their trade designs,

44

Should in their sister's love be blithe and glad,
When 'twas their plan to coax her by degrees
To some high noble and his olive-trees.

XXII

And many a jealous conference had they,
    And many times they bit their lips alone,
Before they fix'd upon a surest way
    To make the youngster for his crime atone;
And at the last, these men of cruel clay
    Cut Mercy with a sharp knife to the bone;
For they resolved in some forest dim
To kill Lorenzo, and there bury him.

XXIII

So on a pleasant morning, as he leant
    Into the sun-rise, o'er the balustrade
Of the garden-terrace, towards him they bent
    Their footing through the dews; and to him said,
'You seem there in the quiet of content,
    Lorenzo, and we are most loth to invade
Calm speculation; but if you are wise,
Bestride your steed while cold is in the skies.

XXIV

'To-day we purpose, aye, this hour we mount
    To spur three leagues towards the Apennine;
Come down, we pray thee, ere the hot sun count
    His dewy rosary on the eglantine.'
Lorenzo, courteously as he was wont,
    Bow'd a fair greeting to these serpents' whine;
And went in haste, to get in readiness,
With belt, and spur, and bracing huntsman's dress.

And as he to the court-yard pass'd along,
  Each third step did he pause, and listen'd oft
If he could hear his lady's matin-song,
  Or the light whisper of her footstep soft;
And as he thus over his passion hung,
  He heard a laugh full musical aloft;
When, looking up, he saw her features bright
Smile through an in-door lattice, all delight.

XXVI

'Love, Isabel!' said he, 'I was in pain
  Lest I should miss to bid thee a good morrow:
Ah! what if I should lose thee, when so fain
  I am to stifle all the heavy sorrow
Of a poor three hours' absence? but we'll gain
  Out of the amorous dark what day doth borrow.
Good bye! I'll soon be back.' – 'Good bye!' said she: –
And as he went she chanted merrily.

XXVII

So the two brothers and their murder'd man
  Rode past fair Florence, to where Arno's stream
Gurgles through straiten'd banks, and still doth fan
  Itself with dancing bulrush, and the bream
Keeps head against the freshets. Sick and wan
  The brothers' faces in the ford did seem,
Lorenzo's flush with love. – They pass'd the water
Into a forest quiet for the slaughter.

XXVIII

There was Lorenzo slain and buried in,
  There in that forest did his great love cease;

Ah! when a soul doth thus its freedom win,
    It aches in loneliness – is ill at peace
As the break-covert blood-hounds of such sin:
    They dipp'd their swords in the water, and did tease
Their horses homeward, with convulsed spur,
Each richer by his being a murderer.

XXIX

They told their sister how, with sudden speed,
    Lorenzo had ta'en ship for foreign lands,
Because of some great urgency and need
    In their affairs, requiring trusty hands.
Poor Girl! put on thy stifling widow's weed,
    And 'scape at once from Hope's accursed bands;
To-day thou wilt not see him, nor to-morrow,
And the next day will be a day of sorrow.

XXX

She weeps alone for pleasures not to be;
    Sorely she wept until the night came on,
And then, instead of love, O misery!
    She brooded o'er the luxury alone:
His image in the dusk she seem'd to see,
    And to the silence made a gentle moan,
Spreading her perfect arms upon the air,
And on her couch low murmuring 'Where? O where?'

XXXI

But Selfishness, Love's cousin, held not long
    Its fiery vigil in her single breast;
She fretted for the golden hour, and hung
    Upon the time with feverish unrest –
Not long – for soon into her heart a throng

Of higher occupants, a richer zest,
Came tragic; passion not to be subdued,
And sorrow for her love in travels rude.

XXXII

In the mid days of autumn, on their eves
  The breath of Winter comes from far away,
And the sick west continually bereaves
  Of some gold tinge, and plays a roundelay
Of death among the bushes and the leaves,
  To make all bare before he dares to stray
From his north cavern. So sweet Isabel
By gradual decay from beauty fell,

XXXIII

Because Lorenzo came not. Oftentimes
  She ask'd her brothers, with an eye all pale,
Striving to be itself, what dungeon climes
  Could keep him off so long? They spake a tale
Time after time, to quiet her. Their crimes
  Came on them, like a smoke from Hinnom's vale;
And every night in dreams they groan'd aloud,
To see their sister in her snowy shroud.

XXXIV

And she had died in drowsy ignorance,
  But for a thing more deadly dark than all;
It came like a fierce potion, drunk by chance,
  Which saves a sick man from the feather'd pall
For some few gasping moments; like a lance,
  Waking an Indian from his cloudy hall
With cruel pierce, and bringing him again
Sense of the gnawing fire at heart and brain.

It was a vision. – In the drowsy gloom,
   The dull of midnight, at her couch's foot
Lorenzo stood, and wept: the forest tomb
   Had marr'd his glossy hair which once could shoot
Lustre into the sun, and put cold doom
   Upon his lips, and taken the soft lute
From his lorn voice, and past his loamed ears
Had made a miry channel for his tears.

Strange sound it was, when the pale shadow spake;
   For there was striving, in its piteous tongue,
To speak as when on earth it was awake,
   And Isabella on its music hung:
Languor there was in it, and tremulous shake,
   As in a palsied Druid's harp unstrung;
And through it moan'd a ghostly under-song,
Like hoarse night-gusts sepulchral briars among.

Its eyes, though wild, were still all dewy bright
   With love, and kept all phantom fear aloof
From the poor girl by magic of their light,
   The while it did unthread the horrid woof
Of the late darken'd time, – the murderous spite
   Of pride and avarice, – the dark pine roof
In the forest, – and the sodden turfed dell,
Where, without any word, from stabs he fell.

Saying moreover, 'Isabel, my sweet!
   Red whortle-berries droop above my head,

And a large flint-stone weighs upon my feet;
    Around me beeches and high chestnuts shed
Their leaves and prickly nuts; a sheep-fold bleat
    Comes from beyond the river to my bed:
Go, shed one tear upon my heather-bloom,
And it shall comfort me within the tomb.

XXXIX

'I am a shadow now, alas! alas!
    Upon the skirts of human-nature dwelling
Alone: I chant alone the holy mass,
    While little sounds of life are round me knelling,
And glossy bees at noon do fieldward pass,
    And many a chapel bell the hour is telling,
Paining me through: those sounds grow strange to me,
And thou art distant in Humanity.

XL

'I know what was, I feel full well what is,
    And I should rage, if spirits could go mad;
Though I forget the taste of earthly bliss,
    That paleness warms my grave, as though I had
A Seraph chosen from the bright abyss
    To be my spouse: thy paleness makes me glad;
Thy beauty grows upon me, and I feel
A greater love through all my essence steal.'

XLI

The Spirit mourn'd 'Adieu!' – dissolv'd, and left
    The atom darkness in a slow turmoil;
As when of healthful midnight sleep bereft,
    Thinking on rugged hours and fruitless toil,
We put our eyes into a pillowy cleft,

And see the spangly gloom froth up and boil:
It made sad Isabella's eyelids ache,
And in the dawn she started up awake;

'Ha! ha!' said she, 'I knew not this hard life,
    I thought the worst was simple misery;
I thought some Fate with pleasure or with strife
    Portion'd us – happy days, or else to die;
But there is crime – a brother's bloody knife!
    Sweet Spirit, thou hast school'd my infancy:
I'll visit thee for this, and kiss thine eyes,
And greet thee morn and even in the skies.'

When the full morning came, she had devised
    How she might secret to the forest hie;
How she might find the clay, so dearly prized,
    And sing to it one latest lullaby;
How her short absence might be unsurmised,
    While she the inmost of the dream would try.
Resolv'd, she took with her an aged nurse,
And went into that dismal forest-hearse.

See, as they creep along the river side,
    How she doth whisper to that aged Dame,
And, after looking round the champaign wide,
    Shows her a knife. – 'What feverous hectic flame
Burns in thee, child? – What good can thee betide,
    That thou should'st smile again?' – The evening came,
And they had found Lorenzo's earthy bed;
The flint was there, the berries at his head.

Who hath not loiter'd in a green church-yard,
    And let his spirit, like a demon-mole,
Work through the clayey soil and gravel hard,
    To see skull, coffin'd bones, and funeral stole;
Pitying each form that hungry Death hath marr'd,
    And filling it once more with human soul?
Ah! this is holiday to what was felt
When Isabella by Lorenzo knelt.

She gaz'd into the fresh-thrown mould, as though
    One glance did fully all its secrets tell;
Clearly she saw, as other eyes would know
    Pale limbs at bottom of a crystal well;
Upon the murderous spot she seem'd to grow,
    Like to a native lily of the dell:
Then with her knife, all sudden, she began
To dig more fervently than misers can.

Soon she turn'd up a soiled glove, whereon
    Her silk had play'd in purple phantasies,
She kiss'd it with a lip more chill than stone,
    And put it in her bosom, where it dries
And freezes utterly unto the bone
    Those dainties made to still an infant's cries:
Then 'gan she work again; nor stay'd her care,
But to throw back at times her veiling hair.

That old nurse stood beside her wondering,
    Until her heart felt pity to the core

At sight of such a dismal labouring,
    And so she kneeled, with her locks all hoar,
And put her lean hands to the horrid thing:
    Three hours they labour'd at this travail sore;
At last they felt the kernel of the grave,
And Isabella did not stamp and rave.

XLIX

Ah! wherefore all this wormy circumstance?
    Why linger at the yawning tomb so long?
O for the gentleness of old Romance,
    The simple plaining of a minstrel's song!
Fair reader, at the old tale take a glance,
    For here, in truth, it doth not well belong
To speak: – O turn thee to the very tale,
And taste the music of that vision pale.

L

With duller steel than the Perséan sword
    They cut away no formless monster's head,
But one, whose gentleness did well accord
    With death, as life. The ancient harps have said,
Love never dies, but lives, immortal Lord:
    If Love impersonate was ever dead,
Pale Isabella kiss'd it, and low moan'd.
'Twas love; cold, – dead indeed, but not dethroned.

LI

In anxious secrecy they took it home,
    And then the prize was all for Isabel:
She calm'd its wild hair with a golden comb,
    And all around each eye's sepulchral cell
Pointed each fringed lash; the smeared loam

With tears, as chilly as a dripping well,
She drench'd away: – and still she comb'd, and kept
Sighing all day – and still she kiss'd, and wept.

LII

Then in a silken scarf, – sweet with the dews
    Of precious flowers pluck'd in Araby,
And divine liquids come with odorous ooze
    Through the cold serpent pipe refreshfully, –
She wrapp'd it up; and for its tomb did choose
    A garden-pot, wherein she laid it by,
And cover'd it with mould, and o'er it set
Sweet Basil, which her tears kept ever wet.

LIII

And she forgot the stars, the moon, and sun,
    And she forgot the blue above the trees,
And she forgot the dells where waters run,
    And she forgot the chilly autumn breeze;
She had no knowledge when the day was done,
    And the new morn she saw not: but in peace
Hung over her sweet Basil evermore,
And moisten'd it with tears unto the core.

LIV

And so she ever fed it with thin tears,
    Whence thick, and green, and beautiful it grew,
So that it smelt more balmy than its peers
    Of Basil-tufts in Florence; for it drew
Nurture besides, and life, from human fears,
    From the fast mouldering head there shut from view:
So that the jewel, safely casketed,
Came forth, and in perfumed leafits spread.

54

O Melancholy, linger here awhile!
    O Music, Music, breathe despondingly!
O Echo, Echo, from some sombre isle,
    Unknown, Lethean, sigh to us – O sigh!
Spirits in grief, lift up your heads, and smile;
    Lift up your heads, sweet Spirits, heavily,
And make a pale light in your cypress glooms,
Tinting with silver wan your marble tombs.

LVI

Moan hither, all ye syllables of woe,
    From the deep throat of sad Melpomene!
Through bronzed lyre in tragic order go,
    And touch the strings into a mystery;
Sound mournfully upon the winds and low;
    For simple Isabel is soon to be
Among the dead: She withers, like a palm
Cut by an Indian for its juicy balm.

LVII

O leave the palm to wither by itself;
    Let not quick Winter chill its dying hour! –
It may not be – those Baälites of pelf,
    Her brethren, noted the continual shower
From her dead eyes; and many a curious elf,
    Among her kindred, wonder'd that such dower
Of youth and beauty should be thrown aside
By one mark'd out to be a Noble's bride.

LVIII

And, furthermore, her brethren wonder'd much
    Why she sat drooping by the Basil green,

And why it flourish'd, as by magic touch;
    Greatly they wonder'd what the thing might mean:
They could not surely give belief, that such
    A very nothing would have power to wean
Her from her own fair youth, and pleasures gay,
And even remembrance of her love's delay.

LIX

Therefore they watch'd a time when they might sift
    This hidden whim; and long they watch'd in vain;
For seldom did she go to chapel-shrift,
    And seldom felt she any hunger-pain;
And when she left, she hurried back, as swift
    As bird on wing to breast its eggs again;
And, patient as a hen-bird, sat her there
Beside her Basil, weeping through her hair.

LX

Yet they contriv'd to steal the Basil-pot,
    And to examine it in secret place:
The thing was vile with green and livid spot,
    And yet they knew it was Lorenzo's face:
The guerdon of their murder they had got,
    And so left Florence in a moment's space,
Never to turn again. – Away they went,
With blood upon their heads, to banishment.

LXI

O Melancholy, turn thine eyes away!
    O Music, Music, breathe despondingly!
O Echo, Echo, on some other day,
    From isles Lethean, sigh to us – O sigh!
Spirits of grief, sing not your 'Well-a-way!'

For Isabel, sweet Isabel, will die;
Will die a death too lone and incomplete,
Now they have ta'en away her Basil sweet.

LXII

Piteous she look'd on dead and senseless things,
    Asking for her lost Basil amorously:
And with melodious chuckle in the strings
    Of her lorn voice, she oftentimes would cry
After the Pilgrim in his wanderings,
    To ask him where her Basil was; and why
'Twas hid from her: 'For cruel 'tis,' said she,
To steal my Basil-pot away from me.'

LXIII

And so she pined, and so she died forlorn,
    Imploring for her Basil to the last.
No heart was there in Florence but did mourn
    In pity of her love, so overcast.
And a sad ditty of this story born
    From mouth to mouth through all the country pass'd:
Still is the burthen sung – 'O cruelty,
To steal my Basil-pot away from me!'

As Keats nursed Tom and his poems in Devon, their more practical and resourceful brother George was attempting to improve
his similarly bleak financial outlook. George found it difficult
to settle on a career, had briefly worked at his guardian Abbey's
tea-business, and entered into a few bad investments that had
already drawn deep on the brothers' scant funds. But George
had fallen in love with a girl called Georgiana Wylie, and they
planned to marry in the spring of 1818, before starting a new life
in America. Keats obviously wished his brother well, and took

immediately to Georgiana, to whom he dedicated a number of poems. But he could see the tight family bond which he had celebrated in his early poem 'To My Brothers' fragmenting, as the newlyweds departed in June 1818. George would never see Tom again, and would see Keats only once and then briefly. Keats felt this separation keenly.

To My Brothers

Small, busy flames play through the fresh laid coals,
  And their faint cracklings o'er our silence creep
  Like whispers of the household gods that keep
A gentle empire o'er fraternal souls.
And while, for rhymes, I search around the poles,
  Your eyes are fix'd, as in poetic sleep,
  Upon the lore so voluble and deep,
That aye at fall of night our care condoles.
This is your birth-day Tom, and I rejoice
  That thus it passes smoothly, quietly.
Many such eves of gently whisp'ring noise
  May we together pass, and calmly try
What are this world's true joys, – ere the great voice
  From its fair face, shall bid our spirits fly.

As George departed for the New World, Keats and his companion Charles Armitage Brown set out on their summer holiday, a walking tour of the Scottish Highlands. Brown was possibly Keats's closest friend in the years 1818–20, and his abortive biography would prove invaluable for piecing together the poet's most important years. He would shortly become his friend's landlord and housemate at Wentworth Place, the Hampstead house that now bears Keats's name. Brown owned half the house (the other half belonging to Charles Wentworth Dilke), and he rented his part out each summer while he travelled. Brown, who was Scottish, planned to explore most of his homeland on foot, and Keats was happy to join him.

Travel was regarded as a form of instruction at the time, and no polite education, and certainly none fostering poetic ambitions, could be considered complete without a tour of the Continent and especially the sites of Classical antiquity. When Keats set out for Scotland via the Lake District he considered this a 'sort of Prologue to the Life I intend to pursue – that is to write, to study, and to see all Europe at the lowest expence'. A 'cockney Homer' (as hostile reviewers would derisively depict him) must perforce take a budget Grand Tour.

And so, on 24th June, they parted from George and Georgiana at Liverpool: the newlyweds to cross the Atlantic, Keats and Brown towards the Lake District, and Wordsworth country where they attempt to visit the Great Man. Keats is appalled to find the once revolutionary poet, who had overturned the poetic world with his and Coleridge's *Lyrical Ballads* in 1798, was out canvassing for the local Tory candidate. They then push north. Their plans were ambitious, even for seasoned walkers, but the terrain was harsh, and the weather worse. The rain that had forced Keats inside in Devon, now delayed or deluged their slow progress around the Highlands and Islands. They made a diversion to Northern Ireland, but found the poverty worse and the weather equal to what they had experienced in Scotland. The Scottish tour fostered but failed to produce much publishable poetry (probably due to the demands of the tour). Fingal's Cave Keats found truly inspiring, discovering a rich vein of Titanic imagery that he would mine in *Hyperion*, the new epic that was shaping in his imagination. And although Robert Burns's cottage proved something of a disappointment for the admiring Keats (having turned into a whisky shop run by a boring sot), it did inspire some of the best lines directly from the tour.

This mortal body of
a thousand days

This mortal body of a thousand days
  Now fills, O Burns, a space in thine own room,
Where thou didst dream alone on budded bays,
  Happy and thoughtless of thy day of doom!
My pulse is warm with thine own Barley-bree,
  My head is light with pledging a great soul,
My eyes are wandering, and I cannot see,
  Fancy is dead and drunken at its goal;
Yet can I stamp my foot upon thy floor,
  Yet can I ope thy window-sash to find
The meadow thou has tramped o'er and o'er, –
  Yet can I think of thee till thought is blind, –
Yet can I gulp a bumper to thy name, –
O smile among the shades, for this is fame!

A rather bleak and rueful perspective on what Keats desired more than anything: literary fame. Keats had and would soon have greater cause to brood darkly on mortality and fame. He had been plagued with a persistent sore throat throughout much of the tour, exacerbated by the weather, cheap lodgings, bad food and the gruelling itinerary. At one point they found themselves wading through bogs in icy rain, hardly conducive to health or comfort for even the stoutest constitution. By early August his chill had worsened, and he was advised by a doctor to return to London. He reached Hampstead on 18th August, foot-sore, weather-beaten, and far from well, only to discover that Tom was worse. He was in fact dying.

Keats took over the full-time nursing of his brother, as he had of his mother just eight years before. September unleashed a further plague on Keats with the long-anticipated (and feared) reviews of *Endymion*. *Blackwoods Magazine* had already attacked

Hunt as leader of a 'cockney' school of poetry, characterised by its vulgarity and insolent rejection of supposed poetic decorum, and had hinted that Keats would be dealt with in due course. It was now his turn. *Blackwoods'* review (of both *Poems* and *Endymion*) styled Keats as a 'cockney' upstart, and protégé of Hunt. It scorned Keats's lack of education and doubted his true understanding of the Greeks he had the temerity to emulate, and concluded with the moral that 'It is a better and a wiser thing to be a starved apothecary than a starved poet,' and exhorted Keats to go 'back to the shop Mr John'. In short, to know his social place. Its author (John Gibson Lockhart) had learned of Keats's origins by the well-meaning but naive efforts of Bailey, who had hoped to forestall such viciousness by appealing to the critic's more charitable side. In vain, for this simply fuelled the class prejudices of the Tory magazine. Cockney apothecaries who 'lisp sedition' were not admitted to the oligarchy of letters.

The 'cockney' slur was repeated by *The Quarterly Review*. Less directly personal than Lockhart, it also denounced Keats for getting above his station. The *Quarterly* was owned by John Murray, the publisher of Lord Byron, Jane Austen and Walter Scott, and later the Brontë sisters, Charles Darwin, John Betjeman and other luminaries. Yet Murray could evidently lack judgment, and personally briefed the reviewer John Wilson Crocker on how Keats 'is thought to possess some talent totally misdirected if not destroyed by the tuition of Leigh Hunt'. For the literary establishment this was sufficient provocation to destroy a fledgling talent.

Keats made light of these criticisms to his friends, fully aware that his poems fell short of the ideal he was now pursuing: 'Praise or blame has but a momentary effect on the man whose love of beauty in the abstract makes him a severe critic on his own Works,' he told his publisher Hessey in October 1818. And yet he must have reeled from the more personal assaults, aimed at the Achilles heel of his social origins. Keats could distance himself from Hunt (as he had done), and could purge his verse of the 'vulgarities' the reviewers associated with his patron or attributed to his lack of education (as he was steadily doing through his own acute discernment); but he could not change his origins or re-write his history. As he once wryly observed, 'You see what it is to be under six foot and not a lord.' He felt such distinctions acutely.

It is fitting that Lord Byron himself would pen the most famous lines concerning the myth that these attacks (including those by his own publisher's bully boy) were later responsible for Keats's death.

> *John Keats, who was killed off by one critique,*
> *Just as he really promised something great,*
> *If not intelligible, – without Greek*
> > *Contrived to talk about the Gods of late,*
> *Much as they might have been supposed to speak.*
> > *Poor fellow! His was an untoward fate: –*
> *'Tis strange the mind, that very fiery particle,*
> *Should let itself be snuffed out by an Article.*
> – Lord Byron, *Don Juan*, XI, 60

Criticism didn't kill Keats, consumption did. The disease that on 1st December claimed the life of his dear brother Tom. He passed away in the early hours, aged just nineteen. Keats went straight to Wentworth Place to break the news to Brown, and became Brown's housemate thereafter.

With Tom gone and George in America, Keats must have felt newly orphaned. His poetic ambitions pilloried in public, his hope for sales dashed by such influential defamation, his prospects were at a very low ebb that winter. Yet the death of Tom and the moving to Wentworth Place mark a turning point in the life, if not the legend, of Keats the Poet. Released from the tender necessity of nursing his brother, he could throw himself into the creation of poetry as he had thrown himself into its study on the death of his mother. As the year turned, it turned into what has come to be known as Keats's 'living year', when he would create the poems that have made him immortal, and experience the love that has made him a myth. This 'living year' would nearly be his last, and is ironically termed. For the tubercle bacillus was no doubt already in his system passed on by Tom, and was slowly drawing him towards his own life's end.

Autumn

By Christmas 1818 Keats had probably fallen in love. It is hard to be certain, because the early days of his relationship with Fanny Brawne, the 'Bright Star' of his tortured, tragic devotion, are shrouded in uncertainty, evasion and ambivalence on his part. They met some time in the late autumn of 1818 at Charles Dilke's side of the house. Keats first mentions Fanny in a letter to his brother and sister-in-law in America started 16th December 1818:

> Mrs Brawne who took Brown's house for the Summer, still resides in Hampstead – she is a very nice woman and her daughter senior is I think beautiful, elegant, graceful, silly, fashionable and strange... monstrous in her behaviour flying out in all directions, calling people such names – that I was forced lately to make use of the term *Minx* – this is I think [not] from any innate vice but from a penchant she has for acting stylishly. I am however tired of such style and shall decline any more of it –

Not the most promising start to a passion that would later consume him body and soul. His account differs markedly from Fanny's own version of events. She claimed the Christmas Day they spent together that year (when they revealed their feelings and entered into a secret understanding) was 'the happiest day

I had ever then spent'. Keats, however, appears to have been keeping his cool. Why?

As we know from Jane Austen (who had died just over a year before), love meant marriage and children, and that required a more regular income. Keats, the poet of intense Sensibility, also had enough practical Sense to understand that his poetic ambitions and his passion probably led in different directions. He could not support himself with his writings, let alone a wife and family. His friend John Hamilton Reynolds was hailed as a poet of great promise alongside Keats and Shelley in Hunt's effusive notice of December 1816; and yet just a year later Reynolds was engaged, and had been compelled by his fiancée to abandon literature for the law. Keats once confessed to not having 'a right feeling towards Women', and in October 1818 he wrote to George, 'I hope I shall never marry. Though the most beautiful Creature were waiting for me at the end of a Journey or a Walk... I should not feel – or rather my Happiness would not be so fine, as my Solitude is sublime... The mighty abstract Idea I have of Beauty in all things stifles the more divided and minute domestic happiness...' This was his refrain throughout the year that followed, as he struggled to reconcile his feelings for Fanny with his material circumstances and his mighty ambitions.

This is not to say Keats was indifferent to the charms of woman, including the physical charms. Sexuality spills out in his poems, and can be glimpsed between the lines of his letters. It was this that a hostile reviewer of *Endymion* objected to most when, in June 1818, he accused Keats of palming 'upon the unsuspicious and the innocent imaginations [material] better adapted to the stews'. Pornography, in other words. 'Stews' is a term for brothel, and it would appear that Keats was not unacquainted with such establishments. He may even have contracted a venereal disease at one (perhaps another reason for his 'not right' view of women). In October 1817 he wrote to Bailey, the Oxford student who would soon be a curate and later an archdeacon, that the 'little Mercury I have taken has corrected the Poison and improved my Health'. Mercury, although not exclusively used to treat syphilis, was generally associated with that disease, and was often used as a euphemism for it from at least the Restoration. To evoke it without clarification in this context implies a shared understanding of the likely nature of this indisposition. Young men visiting prostitutes was simply a fact of life then, when pre-nuptial intercourse was a near impossibility for their class.

Keats's apparent ambivalence to Fanny Brawne may also be partly attributed to a possible rival claimant to his desires. Keats had met Mrs Isabella Jones at Hastings in the spring of 1817, and appears to have become infatuated with her. She was still on the scene two years later. Indeed, when Keats declared to his brother in October 1818 how he did not intend to marry, Isabella may well have been the 'beautiful creature' he was thinking about, as these thoughts come directly after telling George how he had bumped into her in London, accompanied her home and tried to kiss her. Whatever the true extent of their continuing intimacy, it was Isabella who suggested the subject for the poem that heralds the start of Keats's great blossoming. 'The Eve of St Agnes' falls on 20th January, and around that date in 1819 Isabella suggested Keats write a poem dramatising the romantic superstition associated with that date. That,

> ... upon St Agnes' Eve,
> Young virgins might have visions of delight,
> And soft adorings from their loves receive
> Upon the honey'd middle of the night...

This forms the kernel of what is arguably his first completely assured narrative performance, and perhaps the first quintessentially 'Keatsian' poem. By this I mean the emergence, or rather the more controlled expression, of an intense sensualism and rich pictorialism that we now identify as his own. These qualities had been in abundance before, but their luxuriant excess, often for its own decorative sake, generally undermined argument or narrative. Here, finally, they are completely and successfully integral to his design. The very first lines seize the reader's imagination and plunge it into a world of evocative feeling:

> *St Agnes' Eve – Ah, bitter chill it was!*
> *The owl, for all his feathers, was a-cold;*
> *The hare limp'd trembling through the frozen grass,*
> *And silent was the flock in woolly fold:*

Image is piled upon image – frosted breath like incense, statues of knights imagined 'aching' in 'icy hoods and mails' – to establish feelingly a time-frozen, hostile world which he will melt calculatedly by letting the warm love in, in the poetic climax of the bedroom scene. As Porphyro seduces Madeline, with his spiced dainties and honeyed words, so Keats seduces the reader with his richly bejewelled inventiveness, and the gossamer figurativeness of his allusions:

> *Ethereal, flush'd, and like a throbbing star*
> *Seen mid the sapphire heaven's deep repose;*
> *Into her dream he melted, as the rose*
> *Blendeth its odour with the violet, –*
> *Solution sweet...*

With the consummation of Porphyro's passion came the first flush of Keats's maturity, and the first definitive stamp of a characteristic greatness. It was such scenes of richly coloured voluptuousness that attracted the Pre-Raphaelite painters (founded 1848) to a poet they deified, bringing his word-painting to luminous life and his visions to the first generation to recognise Keats's genius. Pictorial yet also purposeful: the narrative flows, the drama sustains, and Keats manages a coherent synthesis of style and subject for the very first time.

The Eve of
St Agnes

I

St Agnes' Eve – Ah, bitter chill it was!
The owl, for all his feathers, was a-cold;
The hare limp'd trembling through the frozen grass,
And silent was the flock in woolly fold:
Numb were the Beadsman's fingers, while he told
His rosary, and while his frosted breath,
Like pious incense from a censer old,
Seem'd taking flight for heaven, without a death,
Past the sweet Virgin's picture, while his prayer he saith.

II

His prayer he saith, this patient, holy man;
Then takes his lamp, and riseth from his knees,
And back returneth, meagre, barefoot, wan,
Along the chapel aisle by slow degrees:
The sculptur'd dead, on each side, seem to freeze,
Emprison'd in black, purgatorial rails:
Knights, ladies, praying in dumb orat'ries,
He passeth by; and his weak spirit fails
To think how they may ache in icy hoods and mails.

III

Northward he turneth through a little door,
And scarce three steps, ere Music's golden tongue
Flatter'd to tears this aged man and poor;
But no – already had his deathbell rung:
The joys of all his life were said and sung:
His was harsh penance on St Agnes' Eve:
Another way he went, and soon among

Rough ashes sat he for his soul's reprieve,
And all night kept awake, for sinners' sake to grieve.

IV

That ancient Beadsman heard the prelude soft;
And so it chanc'd, for many a door was wide,
From hurry to and fro. Soon, up aloft,
The silver, snarling trumpets 'gan to chide:
The level chambers, ready with their pride,
Were glowing to receive a thousand guests:
The carved angels, ever eager-eyed,
Star'd, where upon their heads the cornice rests,
With hair blown back, and wings put cross-wise on their breasts.

V

At length burst in the argent revelry,
With plume, tiara, and all rich array,
Numerous as shadows haunting faerily
The brain, new stuff'd, in youth, with triumphs gay
Of old romance. These let us wish away,
And turn, sole-thoughted, to one Lady there,
Whose heart had brooded, all that wintry day,
On Love, and wing'd St Agnes' saintly care,
As she had heard old dames full many times declare.

VI

They told her how, upon St Agnes' Eve,
Young virgins might have visions of delight,
And soft adorings from their loves receive
Upon the honey'd middle of the night,
If ceremonies due they did aright;
As, supperless to bed they must retire,
And couch supine their beauties, lilly white;

Nor look behind, nor sideways, but require
Of Heaven, with upward eyes for all that they desire.

VII

Full of this whim was thoughtful Madeline:
The music, yearning like a God in pain,
She scarcely heard: her maiden eyes divine,
Fix'd on the floor, saw many a sweeping train
Pass by – she heeded not at all: in vain
Came many a tiptoe, amorous cavalier,
And back retir'd; not cool'd by high disdain,
But she saw not: her heart was otherwhere:
She sigh'd for Agnes' dreams, the sweetest of the year.

She danc'd along with vague, regardless eyes,
Anxious her lips, her breathing quick and short:
The hallow'd hour was near at hand: she sighs
Amid the timbrels, and the throng'd resort
Of whisperers in anger, or in sport;
'Mid looks of love, defiance, hate, and scorn,
Hoodwink'd with faery fancy; all amort,
Save to St Agnes and her lambs unshorn,
And all the bliss to be before to-morrow morn.

IX

So, purposing each moment to retire,
She linger'd still. Meantime, across the moors,
Had come young Porphyro, with heart on fire
For Madeline. Beside the portal doors,
Buttress'd from moonlight, stands he, and implores
All saints to give him sight of Madeline,
But for one moment in the tedious hours,

That he might gaze and worship all unseen;
Perchance speak, kneel, touch, kiss –
in sooth such things have been.

X

He ventures in: let no buzz'd whisper tell:
All eyes be muffled, or a hundred swords
Will storm his heart, Love's fev'rous citadel:
For him, those chambers held barbarian hordes,
Hyena foemen, and hot-blooded lords,
Whose very dogs would execrations howl
Against his lineage: not one breast affords
Him any mercy, in that mansion foul,
Save one old beldame, weak in body and in soul.

XI

Ah, happy chance! The aged creature came,
Shuffling along with ivory-headed wand,
To where he stood, hid from the torch's flame,
Behind a broad hall-pillar, far beyond
The sound of merriment and chorus bland:
He startled her; but soon she knew his face,
And grasp'd his fingers in her palsied hand,
Saying: 'Mercy, Porphyro! hie thee from this place:
They are all here to-night, the whole blood-thirsty race!

XII

'Get hence! get hence! there's dwarfish Hildebrand;
He had a fever late, and in the fit
He cursed thee and thine, both house and land:
Then there's that old Lord Maurice, not a whit
More tame for his gray hairs – Alas me! flit!
Flit like a ghost away.' – 'Ah, Gossip dear,

72

We're safe enough; here in this arm-chair sit,
And tell me how' – 'Good Saints! not here, not here;
Follow me, child, or else these stones will be thy bier.'

XIII

He follow'd through a lowly arched way,
Brushing the cobwebs with his lofty plume,
And as she mutter'd 'Well-a – well-a-day!'
He found him in a little moonlight room,
Pale, lattic'd, chill, and silent as a tomb.
'Now tell me where is Madeline,' said he,
'O tell me, Angela, by the holy loom
Which none but secret sisterhood may see,
When they St Agnes' wool are weaving piously.'

XIV

'St Agnes! Ah! it is St Agnes' Eve –
Yet men will murder upon holy days:
Thou must hold water in a witch's sieve,
And be liege-lord of all the Elves and Fays,
To venture so: it fills me with amaze
To see thee, Porphyro! – St Agnes' Eve!
God's help! my fair lady the conjuror plays
This very night; good angels her deceive!
But let me laugh awhile, I've mickle time to grieve.'

XV

Feebly she laugheth in the languid moon,
While Porphyro upon her face doth look,
Like puzzled urchin on an aged crone
Who keepeth clos'd a wond'rous riddle-book,
As spectacled she sits in chimney nook.
But soon his eyes grew brilliant, when she told

73

His lady's purpose; and he scarce could brook
Tears, at the thought of those enchantments cold,
And Madeline asleep in lap of legends old.

Sudden a thought came like a full-blown rose,
Flushing his brow, and in his pained heart
Made purple riot: then doth he propose
A stratagem, that makes the beldame start:
'A cruel man and impious thou art:
Sweet lady, let her pray, and sleep, and dream
Alone with her good angels, far apart
From wicked men like thee. Go, go! – I deem
Thou canst not surely be the same that thou didst seem.'

XVII

'I will not harm her, by all saints I swear,'
Quoth Porphyro: 'O may I ne'er find grace
When my weak voice shall whisper its last prayer,
If one of her soft ringlets I displace,
Or look with ruffian passion in her face:
Good Angela, believe me by these tears;
Or I will, even in a moment's space,
Awake, with horrid shout, my foemen's ears,
And beard them, though they be more fang'd than
wolves and bears.'

XVIII

'Ah! why wilt thou affright a feeble soul?
A poor, weak, palsy-stricken, churchyard thing,
Whose passing-bell may ere the midnight toll;
Whose prayers for thee, each morn and evening,
Were never miss'd.' – Thus plaining, doth she bring

A gentler speech from burning Porphyro;
So woful, and of such deep sorrowing,
That Angela gives promise she will do
Whatever he shall wish, betide her weal or woe.

XIX

Which was, to lead him, in close secrecy,
Even to Madeline's chamber, and there hide
Him in a closet, of such privacy
That he might see her beauty unespied,
And win perhaps that night a peerless bride,
While legion'd faeries pac'd the coverlet,
And pale enchantment held her sleepy-eyed.
Never on such a night have lovers met,
Since Merlin paid his Demon all the monstrous debt.

XX

'It shall be as thou wishest,' said the Dame:
'All cates and dainties shall be stored there
Quickly on this feast-night: by the tambour frame
Her own lute thou wilt see: no time to spare,
For I am slow and feeble, and scarce dare
On such a catering trust my dizzy head.
Wait there, my child, with patience; kneel in prayer
The while: Ah! Thou must needs the lady wed,
Or may I never leave my grave among the dead.'

XXI

So saying, she hobbled off with busy fear.
The lover's endless minutes slowly pass'd;
The dame return'd, and whisper'd in his ear,
To follow her; with aged eyes aghast
From fright of dim espial. Safe at last,

Through many a dusky gallery, they gain
The maiden's chamber, silken, hush'd, and chaste;
Where Porphyro took covert, pleas'd amain.
His poor guide hurried back with agues in her brain.

XXII

Her falt'ring hand upon the balustrade,
Old Angela was feeling for the stair,
When Madeline, St Agnes' charmed maid,
Rose, like a mission'd spirit, unaware:
With silver taper's light, and pious care,
She turn'd, and down the aged gossip led
To a safe level matting. Now prepare,
Young Porphyro, for gazing on that bed;
She comes, she comes again, like ring-dove fray'd and fled.

XXIII

Out went the taper as she hurried in;
Its little smoke, in pallid moonshine, died:
She clos'd the door, she panted, all akin
To spirits of the air, and visions wide:
No uttered syllable, or, woe betide!
But to her heart, her heart was voluble,
Paining with eloquence her balmy side;
As though a tongueless nightingale should swell
Her throat in vain, and die, heart-stifled, in her dell.

XXIV

A casement high and triple-arch'd there was,
All garlanded with carven imag'ries
Of fruit and flowers, and bunches of knot-grass,
And diamonded with panes of quaint device,
Innumerable of stains and splendid dyes,

As are the tiger-moth's deep-damask'd wings;
And in the midst, 'mong thousand heraldries,
And twilight saints, and dim emblazonings,
A shielded scutcheon blush'd with blood of queens and kings.

XXV

Full on this casement shone the wintry moon,
And threw warm gules on Madeline's fair breast,
As down she knelt for heaven's grace and boon;
Rose-bloom fell on her hands, together prest,
And on her silver cross soft amethyst,
And on her hair a glory, like a saint:
She seem'd a splendid angel, newly drest,
Save wings, for heaven: – Porphyro grew faint:
She knelt, so pure a thing, so free from mortal taint.

XXVI

Anon his heart revives: her vespers done,
Of all its wreathed pearls her hair she frees;
Unclasps her warmed jewels one by one;
Loosens her fragrant boddice; by degrees
Her rich attire creeps rustling to her knees:
Half-ridden, like a mermaid in sea-weed,
Pensive awhile she dreams awake, and sees,
In fancy, fair St Agnes in her bed,
But dares not look behind, or all the charm is fled.

XXVII

Soon, trembling in her soft and chilly nest,
In sort of wakeful swoon, perplex'd she lay,
Until the poppied warmth of sleep oppress'd
Her soothed limbs, and soul fatigued away;
Flown, like a thought, until the morrow-day;

77

Blissfully haven'd both from joy and pain;
Clasp'd like a missal where swart Paynims pray;
Blinded alike from sunshine and from rain,
As though a rose should shut, and be a bud again.

XXVIII

Stol'n to this paradise, and so entranced,
Porphyro gazed upon her empty dress,
And listen'd to her breathing, if it chanced
To wake into a slumberous tenderness;
Which when he heard, that minute did he bless,
And breath'd himself: then from the closet crept,
Noiseless as fear in a wide wilderness,
And over the hush'd carpet, silent, stept,
And 'tween the curtains peep'd, where, lo! – how fast she slept.

XXIX

Then by the bed-side, where the faded moon
Made a dim, silver twilight, soft he set
A table, and, half-anguish'd, threw thereon
A cloth of woven crimson, gold, and jet: –
O for some drowsy Morphean amulet!
The boisterous, midnight, festive clarion,
The kettle-drum, and far-heard clarinet,
Affray his ears, though but in dying tone: –
The hall door shuts again, and all the noise is gone.

XXX

And still she slept an azure-lidded sleep,
In blanched linen, smooth, and lavender'd,
While he from forth the closet brought a heap
Of candied apple, quince, and plum, and gourd;
With jellies soother than the creamy curd,

And lucent syrops, tinct with cinnamon;
Manna and dates, in argosy transferr'd
From Fez; and spiced dainties, every one,
From silken Samarcand to cedar'd Lebanon.

XXXI

These delicates he heap'd with glowing hand
On golden dishes and in baskets bright
Of wreathed silver: sumptuous they stand
In the retired quiet of the night,
Filling the chilly room with perfume light. –
'And now, my love, my seraph fair, awake!
Thou art my heaven, and I thine eremite:
Open thine eyes, for meek St Agnes' sake,
Or I shall drowse beside thee, so my soul doth ache.'

XXXII

Thus whispering, his warm, unnerved arm
Sank in her pillow. Shaded was her dream
By the dusk curtains: – 'twas a midnight charm
Impossible to melt as iced stream:
The lustrous salvers in the moonlight gleam;
Broad golden fringe upon the carpet lies:
It seem'd he never, never could redeem
From such a stedfast spell his lady's eyes;
So mus'd awhile, entoil'd in woofed phantasies.

XXXIII

Awakening up, he took her hollow lute, –
Tumultuous, – and, in chords that tenderest be,
He play'd an ancient ditty, long since mute,
In Provence call'd, 'La belle dame sans mercy':
Close to her ear touching the melody;

Wherewith disturb'd, she utter'd a soft moan:
He ceased – she panted quick – and suddenly
Her blue affrayed eyes wide open shone:
Upon his knees he sank, pale as smooth-sculptured stone.

XXXIV

Her eyes were open, but she still beheld,
Now wide awake, the vision of her sleep:
There was a painful change, that nigh expell'd
The blisses of her dream so pure and deep
At which fair Madeline began to weep,
And moan forth witless words with many a sigh;
While still her gaze on Porphyro would keep;
Who knelt, with joined hands and piteous eye,
Fearing to move or speak, she look'd so dreamingly.

XXXV

Ah, Porphyro!' said she, 'but even now
Thy voice was at sweet tremble in mine ear,
Made tuneable with every sweetest vow;
And those sad eyes were spiritual and clear:
How chang'd thou art! how pallid, chill, and drear!
Give me that voice again, my Porphyro,
Those looks immortal, those complainings dear!
Oh leave me not in this eternal woe,
For if thou diest, my Love, I know not where to go.'

XXXVI

Beyond a mortal man impassion'd far
At these voluptuous accents, he arose,
Ethereal, flush'd, and like a throbbing star
Seen mid the sapphire heaven's deep repose;
Into her dream he melted, as the rose

Blendeth its odour with the violet, –
Solution sweet: meantime the forst-wind blows
Like Love's alarum pattering the sharp sleet
Against the window-panes; St Agnes' moon hath set.

XXXVII

'Tis dark: quick pattereth the flaw-blown sleet:
'This is no dream, my bride, my Madeline!'
'Tis dark: the iced gusts still rave and beat:
'No dream, alas! alas! and woe is mine!
Porphyro will leave me here to fade and pine. –
Cruel! what traitor could thee hither bring?
I curse not, for my heart is lost in thine,
Though thou forsakest a deceived thing; –
A dove forlorn and lost with sick unpruned wing.'

XXXVIII

'My Madeline! sweet dreamer! lovely bride!
Say, may I be for aye thy vassal blest?
Thy beauty's shield, heart-shap'd and vermeil dyed?
Ah, silver shrine, here will I take my rest
After so many hours of toil and quest,
A famish'd pilgrim, – sav'd by miracle.
Though I have found, I will not rob thy nest
Saving of thy sweet self; if thou think'st well
To trust, fair Madeline, to no rude infidel.

XXXIX

'Hark! 'tis an elfin-storm from faery land,
Of haggard seeming, but a boon indeed:
Arise – arise! the morning is at hand; –
The bloated wassaillers will never heed: –
Let us away, my love, with happy speed;

There are no ears to hear, or eyes to see, –
Drown'd all in Rhenish and the sleepy mead:
Awake! arise! my love, and fearless be,
For o'er the southern moors I have a home for thee.'

XL

She hurried at his words, beset with fears,
For there were sleeping dragons all around,
At glaring watch, perhaps, with ready spears –
Down the wide stairs a darkling way they found. –
In all the house was heard no human sound.
A chain-droop'd lamp was flickering by each door;
The arras, rich with horseman, hawk, and hound,
Flutter'd in the besieging wind's uproar;
And the long carpets rose along the gusty floor.

XLI

They glide, like phantoms, into the wide hall;
Like phantoms, to the iron porch, they glide;
Where lay the Porter, in uneasy sprawl,
With a huge empty flagon by his side:
The wakeful bloodhound rose, and shook his hide,
But his sagacious eye an inmate owns:
By one, and one, the bolts full easy slide: –
The chains lie silent on the footworn stones; –
The key turns, and the door upon its hinges groans.

XLII

And they are gone: aye, ages long ago
These lovers fled away into the storm.
That night the Baron dreamt of many a woe,
And all his warrior-guests, with shade and form
Of witch, and demon, and large coffin-worm,

Were long be-nightmar'd. Angela the old
Died palsy-twitch'd, with meagre face deform;
The Beadsman, after thousand aves told,
For aye unsought for slept among his ashes cold.

Not every longer poem Keats now turned his hand to so happily did his bidding. Since his return from Scotland he had been working on an even more ambitious project than *Endymion*. *Hyperion* emerged from the perceived ruins of his earlier 'trial', as a conscious correction of its flaws. He told Benjamin Robert Haydon in January 1818 that whilst *Endymion* had 'many bits of a deep and sentimental cast – the nature of *Hyperion* will lead me to treat it in a more naked and grecian Manner – and the march of passion and endeavour will be undeviating'. He knew he had to strip away the sugary superfluities of expression, and move his actors with purposeful, dramatic direction if he was ever going to measure up to the august ideals he had set for his art. And so he adopted a Miltonic blank verse to allow the range and rigour that his similarly Miltonic theme of colossal rebellion required, and set about constructing a new epic edifice through the autumn and winter of 1818–19.

And yet, by April 1819, Keats abandoned his poem in mid sentence. *Hyperion* would remain and be published as 'A Fragment'. Keats would return to the venture as *The Fall of Hyperion: A Dream* that autumn, only to abandon that in turn a few months later. These epic fragments were what he sadly surveyed when, following confirmation of his illness in February 1820, he lamented, 'If I should die... I have left no immortal work behind me – nothing to make my friends proud of my memory.' This is one of the greatest ironies of Keats's life and work; and yet such 'failures' help us to assess his true achievements.

Deep in the shady sadness of a vale
Far sunken from the healthy breath of morn,
Far from the fiery noon, and eve's one star,
Sat gray-hair'd Saturn, quiet as a stone,
Still as the silence round about his lair;
Forest on forest hung about his head
Like cloud on cloud. No stir of air was there,
Not so much life as on a summer's day
Robs not one light seed from the feather'd grass,
But where the dead leaf fell, there did it rest.
A stream went voiceless by, still deadened more
By reason of his fallen divinity
Spreading a shade: the Naiad 'mid her reeds
Press'd her cold finger closer to her lips.

    Along the margin-sand large foot-marks went,
No further than to where his feet had stray'd,
And slept there since. Upon the sodden ground
His old right hand lay nerveless, listless, dead,
Unsceptred; and his realmless eyes were closed;
While his bow'd head seem'd list'ning to the Earth,
His ancient mother, for some comfort yet.

    It seem'd no force could wake him from his place;
But there came one, who with a kindred hand
Touch'd his wide shoulders, after bending low
With reverence, though to one who knew it not.
She was a Goddess of the infant world;
By her stature the tall Amazon
Had stood at pigmy's height: she would have ta'en
Achilles by the hair and bent his neck;
Or with a finger stay'd Ixion's wheel.
Her face was large as that of Memphian sphinx,
Pedestal'd haply in a palace court,
When sages look'd to Egypt for their lore.

But oh! How unlike marble was that face:
How beautiful, if sorrow had not made
Sorrow more beautiful than Beauty's self.
There was a listening fear in her regard,
As if calamity had but begun;
As if the vanward clouds of evil days
Had spent their malice, and the sullen rear
Was with its stored thunder labouring up.
One hand she press'd upon that aching spot
Where beats the human heart, as if just there,
Though an immortal, she felt cruel pain:
The other upon Saturn's bended neck
She laid, and to the level of his ear
Leaning with parted lips, some words she spake
In solemn tenour and deep organ tone:
Some mourning words, which in our feeble tongue
Would come in these like accents; O how frail
To that large utterance of the early Gods!
'Saturn, look up! – though wherefore, poor old King?
I have no comfort for thee, no not one:
I cannot say "O wherefore sleepest thou?"
For heaven is parted from thee, and the earth
Knows thee not, thus afflicted, for a God;
And ocean too, with all its solemn noise,
Has far from thy sceptre pass'd; and all the air
Is emptied of thine hoary majesty.
Thy thunder, conscious of the new command,
Rumbles reluctant o'er our fallen house;
And thy sharp lightning in unpractis'd hands
Scorches and burns our once serene domain.
O aching time! O moments big as years!
All as ye pass swell out the Monstrous truth,
And press it so upon our weary griefs
That unbelief has not a space to breathe.
Saturn, sleep on: – O thoughtless, why did I

Thus violate thy slumberous solitude?
Why should I ope thy melancholy eyes?
Saturn, sleep on! While at thy feet I weep.'

'Brooding' is a term that characterises the atmosphere of the first *Hyperion*, established powerfully in the opening lines. This is a plausibly Miltonic image. Satan broods on his defeat in *Paradise Lost*. Yet Satan, once the brightest of the angels, eventually musters a fiery resolve to avenge himself and confirm his status as Milton's true hero. Keats's fallen ruler remains somewhat static in comparison, seemingly reluctant to rouse himself from the emblem of melancholy he represents here. There is much solemn lament, outweighing what action there is in the fragment Keats produced.

This tone is not so surprising. Much of *Hyperion* was written while Keats nursed Tom through his final months, and was besieged by hostile reviewers. If Saturn remains far from the fiery noon, Keats's outlook must have appeared equally sun-less during the winter months of 1818. And yet Keats was prepared to acknowledge that suffering, to which he was no stranger, had its purpose and could promote the growth of the mind. He declared to his brother in April 1819 that a 'world of Pains and troubles' was like a school to the intelligence, out of which grew 'a Soul'. This principle is demonstrated perfectly in Keats's best works, pre-eminently the Great Odes written around the time he made these claims to George. In this lyric form he found his voice and the perfect vessel for his mature artistry. It was here that he definitively etched his name in stone.

The first is his 'Ode to Psyche', written in April 1819. This address to the goddess of the mind or soul is singularly appropriate, and could be read as an allegory of the direction of Keats's poetry during that spring: from the more dramatic demands of the epic, to the meditative introspection of the lyric. It opens in a familiar landscape, a classic Keatsian bower, identical to countless *Endymion* set pieces. And yet it goes on to renounce such landscapes for a more restricted but rarefied realm. Keats was turning his art into an altar of the imagination, where he would worship his abstract ideal of beauty born of pleasant pain.

Ode to Psyche

O Goddess! hear these tuneless numbers, wrung
    By sweet enforcement and remembrance dear,
And pardon that thy secrets should be sung
    Even into thine own soft-conched ear:
Surely I dreamt to-day, or did I see
    The winged Psyche with awaken'd eyes?
I wander'd in a forest thoughtlessly,
    And, on the sudden, fainting with surprise,
Saw two fair creatures, couched side by side
    In deepest grass, beneath the whisp'ring roof
    Of leaves and trembled blossoms, where there ran
       A brooklet, scarce espied:

'Mid hush'd, cool-rooted flowers, fragrant-eyed,
    Blue, silver-white, and budded Tyrian,
They lay calm-breathing on the bedded grass;
    Their arms embraced, and their pinions too;
    Their lips touch'd not, but had not bade adieu,
As if disjoined by soft-handed slumber,
And ready still past kisses to outnumber
    At tender eye-dawn of aurorean love:
       The winged boy I knew;
But who wast thou, O happy, happy dove?
       His Psyche true!

O latest born and loveliest vision far
    Of all Olympus' faded hierarchy!
Fairer than Phoebe's sapphire-region'd star,

Or Vesper, amorous glow-worm of the sky;
Fairer than these, though temple thou hast none,
Nor altar heap'd with flowers;
Nor virgin-choir to make delicious moan
Upon the midnight hours;
No voice, no lute, no pipe, no incense sweet
From chain-swung censer teeming;
No shrine, no grove, no oracle, no heat
Of pale-mouth'd prophet dreaming.

O brightest! though too late for antique vows,
Too, too late for the fond believing lyre,
When holy were the haunted forest boughs,
Holy the air, the water, and the fire;
Yet even in these days so far retir'd
From happy pieties, thy lucent fans,
Fluttering among the faint Olympians,
I see, and sing, by my own eyes inspir'd.
So let me be thy choir, and make a moan
Upon the midnight hours;
Thy voice, thy lute, thy pipe, thy incense sweet
From swinged censer teeming;
Thy shrine, thy grove, thy oracle, thy heat
Of pale-mouth'd prophet dreaming.

Yes, I will be thy priest, and build a fane
In some untrodden region of my mind,
Where branched thoughts, new grown with pleasant pain,
Instead of pines shall murmur in the wind:
Far, far around shall those dark-cluster'd trees
Fledge the wild-ridged mountains steep by steep;
And there by zephyrs, streams, and birds, and bees,
The moss-lain Dryads shall be lull'd to sleep;
And in the midst of this wide quietness
A rosy sanctuary will I dress

With the wreath'd trellis of a working brain,
  With buds, and bells, and stars without a name,
With all the gardener Fancy e'er could feign,
  Who breeding flowers, will never breed the same:
And there shall be for thee all soft delight
  That shadowy thought can win,
A bright torch, and a casement ope at night,
  To let the warm Love in!

His 'Ode on a Grecian Urn' reinforces this apparent narrowing of focus demanded of the introspective lyric. This time he focuses on a work of art.

Ode on a Grecian Urn

I

Thou still unravish'd bride of quietness,
  Thou foster-child of silence and slow time,
Sylvan historian, who canst thus express
  A flowery tale more sweetly than our rhyme:
What leaf-fring'd legend haunts about thy shape
  Of deities or mortals, or of both,
    In Tempe or the dales of Arcady?
  What men or gods are these? What maidens loth?
What mad pursuits? What struggle to escape?
  What pipes and timbrels? What wild ecstasy?

II

Heard melodies are sweet, but those unheard
  Are sweeter; therefore, ye soft pipes, play on;
Not to the sensual ear, but, more endear'd,
  Pipe to the spirit ditties of no tone:
Fair youth, beneath the trees, thou canst not leave

Thy song, nor ever can those trees be bare;
  Bold Lover, never, never canst thou kiss,
Though winning near the goal – yet, do not grieve;
She cannot fade, though thou hast not thy bliss,
  For ever wilt thou love, and she be fair!

III

Ah, happy, happy boughs! that cannot shed
  Your leaves, nor ever bid the Spring adieu;
And, happy melodist, unwearied,
  For ever piping songs for ever new;
More happy love! more happy, happy love!
  For ever warm and still to be enjoy'd,
    For ever panting, and for ever young;
All breathing human passion far above,
  That leaves a heart high-sorrowful and cloy'd,
    A burning forehead, and a parching tongue.

IV

Who are these coming to the sacrifice?
  To what green altar, O mysterious priest,
Lead'st thou that heifer lowing at the skies,
  And all her silken flanks with garlands drest?
What little town by river or sea shore,
  Or mountain-built with peaceful citadel,
    Is emptied of this folk, this pious morn?
And, little town, thy streets for evermore
  Will silent be; and not a soul to tell
    Why thou art desolate, can e'er return.

V

O Attic shape! Fair attitude! with brede
  Of marble men and maidens overwrought,

With forest branches and the trodden weed;
  Thou, silent form, dost tease us out of thought
As doth eternity: Cold Pastoral!
  When old age shall this generation waste,
    Thou shalt remain, in midst of other woe
Than ours, a friend to man, to whom thou say'st,
  'Beauty is truth, truth beauty,' – that is all
    Ye know on earth, and all ye need to know.

I have suggested that stillness was partly to blame for the abandonment of *Hyperion*, where Saturn and his Giants remain for a long time 'like a stone', to the detriment of dramatic development. Not here. The conceit of describing and addressing a work of art allows the poet to explore a problem – the role of beauty in an imperfect world – with greater concision and control than his earlier 'flowery tales'. Stillness (in time and space) is the Urn's and the Ode's strength. As the bold lover cannot kiss, nor spring turn to summer, so the poet's numerous questions go unanswered. This is what Keats called 'Negative Capability' actualised. This quality (expounded in a letter of December 1817) Keats held as the philosophical ideal of art, and was the state un which a poet was 'capable of being in uncertainties, Mysteries, doubts, without any irritable reaching after fact & reason' in verse. It is turned into a moral as much as an aesthetic ideal in his poem. Withheld facts, unsolved mysteries, unravished brides allow evasion of the ills and pains to which mortal flesh is heir. A 'cold' pastoral perhaps, but a beguiling one.

Spring 1819 is as remarkable for its intensity as for its quality, with all the Great Odes except 'To Autumn' coming in quick succession from the middle of April to the end of May. But why now? Keats was alone as never before, which may have encouraged greater introspection, and been conducive to creativity. He was living with Brown, at Wentworth Place (as a paying lodger), which gave him space and peace close to his beloved

Hampstead Heath. The fine weather might also have played a part. He mentions it in a letter to his sister on 12th April, and again on 1st May, declaring 'O there is nothing like fine weather, and health, and Books, and a fine country and a contented Mind...' Coming after the appalling spring and summer of the year before, the sunlit pastoral world beyond his back door was the cause of discernible relief. This is the world he evokes so feelingly in the most famous poem from this spring, 'Ode to a Nightingale' (originally to 'the' Nightingale), composed under these benign conditions.

Its composition has itself become the stuff of legend, thanks to the account supplied twenty years later by his housemate Brown, who recalls how:

> In the spring of 1819 a nightingale had built her nest near my house. Keats felt a tranquil and continual joy in her song; and one morning he took his chair from the breakfast-table to the grass-plot under a plum-tree, where he sat for two or three hours. When he came into the house, I perceived he had some scraps of paper in his hand, and these he was quietly thrusting behind the books. On inquiry, I found those scraps, four or five in number, contained his poetic feeling on the song of our nightingale. The writing was not well legible; and it was difficult to arrange the stanzas on so many scraps. With his assistance I succeeded, and this was his *Ode to a Nightingale*, a poem which has been the delight of every one. Immediately afterwards I searched for more of his (in reality) fugitive pieces, in which task, at my request, he again assisted me. Thus I rescued that *Ode* and other valuable short poems, which might otherwise have been lost.

It's a captivating (albeit probably apocryphal) image, captured posthumously in the idealised painting by Joseph Severn depicting Keats as the rapt rhapsodist of Brown's anecdote, versifying in careless creative frenzy. Whether true or not, it reinforces the irony that Keats did not think as highly of the lyrics that made him legendary, as of the epic schemes upon which he frustratingly laboured.

Ode to a Nightingale

My heart aches, and a drowsy numbness pains
    My sense, as though of hemlock I had drunk,
Or emptied some dull opiate to the drains
    One minute past, and Lethe-wards had sunk:
'Tis not through envy of thy happy lot,
    But being too happy in thine happiness, –
        That thou, light-winged Dryad of the trees,
            In some melodious plot
    Of beechen green, and shadows numberless,
        Singest of summer in full-throated ease.

II

O, for a draught of vintage! that hath been
    Cool'd a long age in the deep-delved earth,
Tasting of Flora and the country green,
    Dance, and Provençal song, and sunburnt mirth!
O for a beaker full of the warm South,
    Full of the true, the blushful Hippocrene,
        With beaded bubbles winking at the brim,
            And purple-stained mouth;
    That I might drink, and leave the world unseen,
        And with thee fade away into the forest dim:

III

Fade far away, dissolve, and quite forget
    What thou among the leaves hast never known,

The weariness, the fever, and the fret
    Here, where men sit and hear each other groan;
Where palsy shakes a few, sad, last gray hairs,
    Where youth grows pale, and spectre-thin, and dies;
        Where but to think is to be full of sorrow
            And leaden-eyed despairs,
    Where Beauty cannot keep her lustrous eyes,
        Or new Love pine at them beyond to-morrow.

IV

Away! away! for I will fly to thee,
    Not charioted by Bacchus and his pards,
But on the viewless wings of Poesy,
    Though the dull brain perplexes and retards:
Already with thee! tender is the night,
    And haply the Queen-Moon is on her throne,
        Cluster'd around by all her starry Fays;
            But here there is no light,
    Save what from heaven is with the breezes blown
        Through verdurous glooms and winding mossy ways.

V

I cannot see what flowers are at my feet,
    Nor what soft incense hangs upon the boughs,
But, in embalmed darkness, guess each sweet
    Wherewith the seasonable month endows
The grass, the thicket, and the fruit-tree wild;
    White hawthorn, and the pastoral eglantine;
        Fast fading violets cover'd up in leaves;
            And mid-May's eldest child,
    The coming musk-rose, full of dewy wine,
        The murmurous haunt of flies on summer eves.

VI

Darkling I listen; and, for many a time
*   I have been half in love with easeful Death,*
Call'd him soft names in many a mused rhyme,
*   To take into the air my quiet breath;*
Now more than ever seems it rich to die,
*   To cease upon the midnight with no pain,*
*   While thou art pouring forth thy soul abroad*
*   In such an ecstasy!*
*   Still wouldst thou sing, and I have ears in vain –*
*   To thy high requiem become a sod.*

VII

Thou wast not born for death, immortal Bird!
*   No hungry generations tread thee down;*
The voice I hear this passing night was heard
*   In ancient days by emperor and clown:*
Perhaps the self-same song that found a path
*   Through the sad heart of Ruth, when, sick for home,*
*   She stood in tears amid the alien corn;*
*   The same that oft-times hath*
*   Charm'd magic casements, opening on the foam*
*   Of perilous seas, in faery lands forlorn.*

Forlorn! the very word is like a bell
*   To toll me back from thee to my sole self!*
Adieu! the fancy cannot cheat so well
*   As she is fam'd to do, deceiving elf.*
Adieu! adieu! thy plaintive anthem fades
*   Past the near meadows, over the still stream,*
*   Up the hill-side; and now 'tis buried deep*

> *In the next valley-glades:*
> *Was it a vision, or a waking dream?*
> *Fled is that music: – Do I wake or sleep?*

Fine weather may have delighted Keats that spring, but 'the contended mind' he professes to his sister was not as cloudless as the skies, if 'Nightingale' is its faithful record. The soul made from suffering, the verse drawn from that soul dwells as much in dark hollows as in sunlit heights. If the Grecian Urn remained a friend to man by escaping his sad lot, the Nightingale's eternal song merely serves as a reminder of his woes. The dying fall and sense of forlorn desertion of the final stanza offers little succour beyond the ability to experience the beauty of the song or poem in itself. Beauty as a sufficient truth, albeit fleetingly.

Indeed, the 'spring odes', born amid fine weather, are darkly meditative, establishing a new philosophical maturity and their enduring power through their creative engagement with the paradoxes of 'pleasant pain'. His other Great Ode from these weeks does this directly in its celebration of 'Melancholy'. This suggests that joy and melancholy are of a piece, and that the latter is the more exulted or refined state:

Ode on Melancholy

I

> *No, no, go not to Lethe, neither twist*
> *Wolf's-bane, tight-rooted, for its poisonous wine;*
> *Nor suffer thy pale forehead to be kiss'd*
> *By nightshade, ruby grape of Proserpine;*
> *Make not your rosary of yew-berries,*
> *Nor let the beetle, nor the death-moth be*

Your mournful Psyche, nor the downy owl
A partner in your sorrow's mysteries;
  For shade to shade will come too drowsily,
    And drown the wakeful anguish of the soul.

II

But when the melancholy fit shall fall
  Sudden from heaven like a weeping cloud,
That fosters the droop-headed flowers all,
  And hides the green hill in an April shroud;
Then glut thy sorrow on a morning rose,
  Or on the rainbow of the salt sand-wave,
    Or on the wealth of globed peonies;
Or if thy mistress some rich anger shows,
  Emprison her soft hand, and let her rave,
    And feed deep, deep upon her peerless eyes.

III

She dwells with Beauty – Beauty that must die;
  And Joy, whose hand is ever at his lips
Bidding adieu; and aching Pleasure nigh,
  Turning to Poison while the bee-mouth sips:
Ay, in the very temple of delight
  Veil'd Melancholy has her sovran shrine,
Though seen of none save him whose strenuous tongue
  Can burst Joy's grape against his palate fine;
His soul shall taste the sadness of her might,
  And be among her cloudy trophies hung.

The fleeting pleasures of the mutable world, frozen through artifice, in the Urn are evoked once again. But the poet no longer resists fulfilment, embracing the painful pleasures that make a soul. The dark eroticism of the final image is a world away from the clammy adolescent fumblings of *Endymion* – with its 'slippery blisses' etc. – and anticipates the disturbing visions of vampiric sexuality of Symbolist poets like Charles Baudelaire. This note Keats had already struck in his ballad 'La Belle Dame Sans Merci' (written about a month before 'Melancholy'), whose images of erotic enthralment would delight the Symbolist painters of the late nineteenth century as much as his richly coloured romances did the Pre-Raphaelites before.

La Belle Dame Sans Merci. A Ballad

I

Ah, what can ail thee, wretched wight,
*   Alone and palely loitering;*
The sedge is wither'd from the lake,
*   And no birds sing.*

II

Ah, what can ail thee, wretched wight,
*   So haggard and so woe-begone?*
The squirrel's granary is full,
*   And the harvest's done.*

III

I see a lilly on thy brow,
*   With anguish moist and fever dew;*
And on thy cheek a fading rose
*   Fast withereth too.*

IV

I met a lady in the meads
*   Full beautiful, a faery's child;*

Her hair was long, her foot was light,
  And her eyes were wild.

V

I set her on my pacing steed,
  And nothing else saw all day long;
For sideways would she lean, and sing
  A faery's song.

VI

I made a garland for her head,
  And bracelets too, and fragrant zone;
She look'd at me as she did love,
  And made sweet moan.

VII

She found me roots of relish sweet,
  And honey wild, and manna dew;
And sure in language strange she said,
  I love thee true.

VIII

She took me to her elfin grot,
  And there she gaz'd and sighed deep,
And there I shut her wild sad eyes –
  So kiss'd to sleep.

IX

And there we slumber'd on the moss,
  And there I dream'd, ah woe betide,
The latest dream I ever dream'd
  On the cold hill side.

I saw pale kings, and princes too,
Pale warriors, death-pale were they all;
Who cry'd – 'La belle Dame sans merci
Hath thee in thrall!'

I saw their starv'd lips in the gloam
With horrid warning gaped wide,
And I awoke, and found me here
On the cold hill side.

And this is why I sojourn here
Alone and palely loitering,
Though the sedge is wither'd from the lake,
And no birds sing.

The twilit melancholy and sinister eroticism of such poems might tempt us to speculate on Keats's state of mind, and specifically his feelings about Fanny, that spring. April, which brought fine weather and intense creativity, also brought the two lovers closer together. On the 19th, the Dilkes moved out of their half of the house to be closer to their son who was a pupil at Westminster School. As they moved out, so the widowed Mrs Brawne, her son and two daughters moved in. Keats's secret lover was now living under the same roof. Such physical proximity allowed greater intimacy; but Keats appears determined to retain a certain emotional detachment and independence. An abstract ideal of beauty was still his goal, even if this might be taking a more tangible form in his charming young neighbour. When he professes his love to Fanny in his earliest surviving letter to her (dated 1st July 1819), he depicts it as a form of entrapment, not unlike the fate of the 'enthralled' victims of La Belle Dame, or Lady Melancholy's 'trophies'. He challenges the poor girl, 'Ask yourself my love whether you are not very cruel to have so entrammelled me, so destroyed my freedom.' This is partly the approved rhetoric of poetic love (the lover as doting slave), but also partly a sincere expression of frustrated desire and even resentment.

The July letter to Fanny was written from Shanklin, in the Isle of Wight, where Keats spent most of the summer with Brown, as his side of Wentworth Place was rented out for the season once again. Keats appears to have turned the necessity of his enforced sojourn from Hampstead into a virtue by distancing himself and his troubled feelings from Fanny. His letters were infrequent, and in early September, when he was forced to make a flying visit to London (to attempt to release capital for George, whose ventures had foundered in America), he didn't visit her. Instead he wrote her an agonised, confused and confusing letter. Explaining:

> If I were to see you to day it would destroy the half comfortable sullenness I enjoy at present into [downright] perplexities. I love you too much to venture to Hampstead, I feel it is not paying a visit, but venturing into a fire. … Knowing well that my life must be passed in fatigue and trouble, I have been endeavouring to wean myself from you: for to myself alone what can be much of a misery? … I am a Coward, I cannot bear the pain of being happy…

In other words, 'it's not you, it's me.' Comments he made to others on this theme are perhaps more candid in their rejection of domestic 'happiness'. He declared in a letter to his brother not long afterwards how 'Nothing strikes me so forcibly with a sense of the rediculous as love – A Man in love I do think cuts the sorryest figure in the world.' And to his publisher Taylor, how he equally disliked 'the favour of the public with the love of a woman – they are both a cloying treacle to the wings of independence'. The 'happiness' he told Fanny he was afraid of was to his friends a more straightforward lack of independence. He had just found his poetic wings, and was not yet ready to have them clipped or cloyed by love.

Such conflicts are at the heart of 'Lamia', which Keats wrote during his holiday from Hampstead that summer. Rather simplistically, 'Lamia' stages a conflict between competing desires, duties, and modes of thinking, that, like the Odes, he leaves richly unresolved. This conflict is tellingly embodied in the tragic love story of a young student compelled to choose between the (professional) claims of reason, and his personal desires for a beautiful, but potentially sinister temptress. 'Lamia' his lover is, after all, a snake who has been turned into a woman so she can woo Lycius. Such metamorphoses (albeit usually from human to non-human) are the stock of the ancient myths that were Keats's constant models. Yet frequent narratorial intrusions suggest this ancient fable is troubled by more personal concerns. If romantic conflicts leave their mark on his philosophical problem poem, money troubles also appear to creep into the frame. They become the same issue in the lines that open Part II, with a worldly couplet worthy of Byron:

> Love in a hut, with water and a crust,
> Is – Love, forgive us! cinder, ashes, dust;
> Love in a palace is perhaps at last
> More grievous torment than a hermit's fast...

Love in a hut would be exactly their lot if Keats resolved to marry Fanny, spelling the end of his poetic ambitions.

Lamia

Part I

Upon a time, before the faery broods
Drove Nymph and Satyr from the prosperous woods,
Before King Oberon's bright diadem,
Sceptre, and mantle, clasp'd with dewy gem,
Frighted away the Dryads and the Fauns
From rushes green, and brakes, and cowslip'd lawns,
The ever-smitten Hermes empty left
His golden throne, bent warm on amorous theft:
From high Olympus had he stolen light,
On this side of Jove's clouds, to escape the sight
Of his great summoner, and made retreat
Into a forest on the shores of Crete.
For somewhere in that sacred island dwelt
A nymph, to whom all hoofed Satyrs knelt;
At whose white feet the languid Tritons poured
Pearls, while on land they wither'd and adored.
Fast by the springs where she to bathe was wont,
And in those meads where sometime she might haunt,
Were strewn rich gifts, unknown to any Muse,
Though Fancy's casket were unlock'd to choose.
Ah, what a world of love was at her feet!
So Hermes thought, and a celestial heat
Burnt from his winged heels to either ear,
That from a whiteness, as the lilly clear,
Blush'd into roses 'mid his golden hair,
Fallen in jealous curls about his shoulders bare.

From vale to vale, from wood to wood, he flew,
Breathing upon the flowers his passion new,
And wound with many a river to its head,

To find where this sweet nymph prepar'd her secret bed:
In vain; the sweet nymph might nowhere be found,
And so he rested, on the lonely ground,
Pensive, and full of painful jealousies
Of the Wood-Gods, and even the very trees.
There as he stood, he heard a mournful voice,
Such as once heard, in gentle heart, destroys
All pain but pity: thus the lone voice spake:
'When from this wreathed tomb shall I awake!
When move in a sweet body fit for life,
And love, and pleasure, and the ruddy strife
Of hearts and lips! Ah, miserable me!'
The God, dove-footed, glided silently
Round bush and tree, soft-brushing, in his speed,
The taller grasses and full-flowering weed,
Until he found a palpitating snake,
Bright, and cirque-couchant in a dusky brake.

She was a gordian shape of dazzling hue,
Vermilion-spotted, golden, green, and blue;
Striped like a zebra, freckled like a pard,
Eyed like a peacock, and all crimson barr'd;
And full of silver moons, that, as she breathed,
Dissolv'd, or brighter shone, or interwreathed
Their lustres with the gloomier tapestries —
So rainbow-sided, touch'd with miseries,
She seem'd, at once, some penanced lady elf,
Some demon's mistress, or the demon's self.
Upon her crest she wore a wannish fire
Sprinkled with stars, like Ariadne's tiar:
Her head was serpent, but ah, bitter-sweet!
She had a woman's mouth with all its pearls complete:
And for her eyes: what could such eyes do there
But weep, and weep, that they were born so fair?
As Proserpine still weeps for her Sicilian air.

Her throat was serpent, but the words she spake
Came, as through bubbling honey, for Love's sake,
And thus; while Hermes on his pinions lay,
Like a stoop'd falcon ere he takes his prey.

'Fair Hermes, crown'd with feathers, fluttering light,
I had a splendid dream of thee last night:
I saw thee sitting, on a throne of gold,
Among the Gods, upon Olympus old,
The only sad one; for thou didst not hear
The soft, lute-finger'd Muses chaunting clear,
Nor even Apollo when he sang alone,
Deaf to his throbbing throat's long, long melodious moan.
I dreamt I saw thee, robed in purple flakes,
Break amorous through the clouds, as morning breaks,
And, swiftly as a bright Phoebean dart,
Strike for the Cretan isle; and here thou art!
Too gentle Hermes, hast thou found the maid?'
Whereat the star of Lethe not delay'd
His rosy eloquence, and thus inquired:
'Thou smooth-lipp'd serpent, surely high inspired!
Thou beauteous wreath, with melancholy eyes,
Possess whatever bliss thou canst devise,
Telling me only where my nymph is fled, –
Where she doth breathe!' 'Bright planet, thou hast said,'
Return'd the snake, 'but seal with oaths, fair God!'
'I swear,' said Hermes, 'by my serpent rod,
And by thine eyes, and by thy starry crown!'
Light flew his earnest words, among the blossoms blown.
Then thus again the brilliance feminine:
'Too frail of heart! for this lost nymph of thine,
Free as the air, invisibly, she strays
About these thornless wilds; her pleasant days
She tastes unseen; unseen her nimble feet
Leave traces in the grass and flowers sweet;

From weary tendrils, and bow'd branches green,
She plucks the fruit unseen, she bathes unseen:
And by my power is her beauty veil'd
To keep it unaffronted, unassail'd
By the love-glances of unlovely eyes,
Of Satyrs, Fauns, and blear'd Silenus' sighs.
Pale grew her immortality, for woe
Of all these lovers, and she grieved so
I took compassion on her, bade her steep
Her hair in weïrd syrops, that would keep
Her loveliness invisible, yet free
To wander as she loves, in liberty.
Thou shalt behold her, Hermes, thou alone,
If thou wilt, as thou swearest, grant my boon!'
Then, once again, the charmed God began
An oath, and through the serpent's ears it ran
Warm, tremulous, devout, psalterian.
Ravish'd, she lifted her Circean head,
Blush'd a live damask, and swift-lisping said,
'I was a woman, let me have once more
A woman's shape, and charming as before.
I love a youth of Corinth – O the bliss!
Give me my woman's form, and place me where he is.
Stoop, Hermes, let me breathe upon thy brow,
And thou shalt see thy sweet nymph even now.'
The God on half-shut feathers sank serene,
She breath'd upon his eyes, and swift was seen
Of both the guarded nymph near-smiling on the green.
It was no dream; or say a dream it was,
Real are the dreams of Gods, and smoothly pass
Their pleasures in a long immortal dream.
One warm, flush'd moment, hovering, it might seem
Dash'd by the wood-nymph's beauty, so he burn'd;
Then, lighting on the printless verdure, turn'd
To the swoon'd serpent, and with languid arm,

Delicate, put to proof the lythe Caducean charm.
So done, upon the nymph his eyes he bent,
Full of adoring tears and blandishment,
And towards her stept: she, like a moon in wane,
Faded before him, cower'd, nor could restrain
Her fearful sobs, self-folding like a flower
That faints into itself at evening hour:
But the God fostering her chilled hand,
She felt the warmth, her eyelids open'd bland,
And, like new flowers at morning song of bees,
Bloom'd, and gave up her honey to the lees.
Into the green-recessed woods they flew;
Nor grew they pale, as mortal lovers do.

    Left to herself, the serpent now began
To change; her elfin blood in madness ran,
Her mouth foam'd, and the grass, therewith besprent,
Wither'd at dew so sweet and virulent;
Her eyes in torture fix'd, and anguish drear,
Hot, glaz'd, and wide, with lid-lashes all sear,
Flash'd phosphor and sharp sparks, without one cooling tear.
The colours all inflam'd throughout her train,
She writh'd about, convuls'd with scarlet pain:
A deep volcanian yellow took the place
Of all her milder-mooned body's grace;
And, as the lava ravishes the mead,
Spoilt all her silver mail, and golden brede;
Made gloom of all her frecklings, streaks and bars,
Eclips'd her crescents, and lick'd up her stars:
So that, in moments few, she was undrest
Of all her sapphires, greens, and amethyst,
And rubious-argent: of all these bereft,
Nothing but pain and ugliness were left.
Still shone her crown; that vanish'd, also she
Melted and disappear'd as suddenly;

And in the air, her new voice luting soft,
Cried, 'Lycius! gentle Lycius!' – Borne aloft
With the bright mists about the mountains hoar
These words dissolv'd: Crete's forests heard no more.

Whither fled Lamia, now a lady bright,
A full-born beauty new and exquisite?
She fled into that valley they pass o'er
Who go to Corinth from Cenchreas' shore;
And rested at the foot of those wild hills,
The rugged founts of the Peraean rills,
And of that other ridge whose barren back
Stretches, with all its mist and cloudy rack,
South-westward to Cleone. There she stood
About a young bird's flutter from a wood,
Fair, on a sloping green of mossy tread,
By a clear pool, wherein she passioned
To see herself escap'd from so sore ills,
While her robes flaunted with the daffodils.

Ah, happy Lycius! – for she was a maid
More beautiful than ever twisted braid,
Or sigh'd, or blush'd, or on spring-flowered lea
Spread a green kirtle to the minstrelsy:
A virgin purest lipp'd, yet in the lore
Of love deep learned to the red heart's core:
Not one hour old, yet of sciential brain
To unperplex bliss from its neighbour pain;
Define their pettish limits, and estrange
Their points of contact, and swift counterchange;
Intrigue with the specious chaos, and dispart
Its most ambiguous atoms with sure art;
As though in Cupid's college she had spent
Sweet days a lovely graduate, still unshent,
And kept his rosy terms in idle languishment.

Why this fair creature chose so faerily
By the wayside to linger, we shall see;
But first 'tis fit to tell how she could muse
And dream, when in the serpent prison-house,
Of all she list, strange or magnificent:
How, ever, where she will'd, her spirit went;
Whether to faint Elysium, or where
Down through tress-lifting waves the Nereids fair
Wind into Thetis' bower by many a pearly stair;
Or where God Bacchus drains his cups divine,
Stretch'd out, at ease, beneath a glutinous pine;
Or where in Pluto's gardens palatine
Mulciber's columns gleam in far piazzian line.
And sometimes into cities she would send
Her dream, with feast and rioting to blend;
And once, while among mortals dreaming thus,
She saw the young Corinthian Lycius
Charioting foremost in the envious race,
Like a young Jove with calm uneager face,
And fell into a swooning love of him.
Now on the moth-time of that evening dim
He would return that way, as well she knew,
To Corinth from the shore; for freshly blew
The eastern soft wind, and his galley now
Grated the quaystones with her brazen prow
In port Cenchreas, from Egina isle
Fresh anchor'd; whither he had been awhile
To sacrifice to Jove, whose temple there
Waits with high marble doors for blood and incense rare.
Jove heard his vows, and better'd his desire;
For by some freakful chance he made retire
From his companions, and set forth to walk,
Perhaps grown wearied of their Corinth talk:
Over the solitary hills he fared,
Thoughtless at first, but ere eve's star appeared

His phantasy was lost, where reason fades,
In the calm'd twilight of Platonic shades.
Lamia beheld him coming, near, more near –
Close to her passing, in indifference drear,
His silent sandals swept the mossy green;
So neighbour'd to him, and yet so unseen
She stood: he pass'd, shut up in mysteries,
His mind wrapp'd like his mantle, while her eyes
Follow'd his steps, and her neck regal white
Turn'd – syllabling thus, 'Ah, Lycius bright,
And will you leave me on the hills alone?
Lycius, look back! and be some pity shown.'
He did; not with cold wonder fearingly,
But Orpheus-like at an Eurydice;
For so delicious were the words she sung,
It seem'd he had lov'd them a whole summer long:
And soon his eyes had drunk her beauty up,
Leaving no drop in the bewildering cup,
And still the cup was full, – while he afraid
Lest she should vanish ere his lip had paid
Due adoration, thus began to adore;
Her soft look growing coy, she saw his chain so sure:
'Leave thee alone! Look back! Ah, Goddess, see
Whether my eyes can ever turn from thee!
For pity do not this sad heart belie –
Even as thou vanishest so I shall die.
Stay! though a Naiad of the rivers, stay!
To thy far wishes will thy streams obey:
Stay! though the greenest woods be thy domain,
Alone they can drink up the morning rain:
Though a descended Pleiad, will not one
Of thine harmonious sisters keep in tune
Thy spheres, and as thy silver proxy shine?
So sweetly to these ravish'd ears of mine
Came thy sweet greeting, that if thou shouldst fade

Thy memory will waste me to a shade –
For pity do not melt!'– 'If I should stay,'
Said Lamia, 'here, upon this floor of clay,
And pain my steps upon these flowers too rough,
What canst thou say or do of charm enough
To dull the nice remembrance of my home?
Thou canst not ask me with thee here to roam
Over these hills and vales, where no joy is, –
Empty of immortality and bliss!
Thou art a scholar, Lycius, and must know
That finer spirits cannot breathe below
In human climes, and live: Alas! poor youth,
What taste of purer air hast thou to soothe
My essence? What serener palaces,
Where I may all my many senses please,
And by mysterious sleights a hundred thirsts appease?
It cannot be – Adieu!' So said, she rose
Tiptoe with white arms spread. He, sick to lose
The amorous promise of her lone complain,
Swoon'd, murmuring of love, and pale with pain.
The cruel lady, without any show
Of sorrow for her tender favourite's woe,
But rather, if her eyes could brighter be,
With brighter eyes and slow amenity,
Put her new lips to his, and gave afresh
The life she had so tangled in her mesh:
And as he from one trance was wakening
Into another, she began to sing,
Happy in beauty, life, and love, and every thing,
A song of love, too sweet for earthly lyres,
While, like held breath, the stars drew in their panting fires.
And then she whisper'd in such trembling tone,
As those who, safe together met alone
For the first time through many anguish'd days,
Use other speech than looks; bidding him raise

His drooping head, and clear his soul of doubt,
For that she was a woman, and without
Any more subtle fluid in her veins
Than throbbing blood, and that the self-same pains
Inhabited her frail-strung heart as his.
And next she wonder'd how his eyes could miss
Her face so long in Corinth, where, she said,
She dwelt but half retir'd, and there had led
Days happy as the gold coin could invent
Without the aid of love; yet in content
Till she saw him, as once she pass'd him by,
Where 'gainst a column he leant thoughtfully
At Venus' temple porch, 'mid baskets heap'd
Of amorous herbs and flowers, newly reap'd
Late on that eve, as 'twas the night before
The Adonian feast; whereof she saw no more,
But wept alone those days, for why should she adore?
Lycius from death awoke into amaze,
To see her still, and singing so sweet lays;
Then from amaze into delight he fell
To hear her whisper woman's lore so well;
And every word she spake entic'd him on
To unperplex'd delight and pleasure known.
Let the mad poets say whate'er they please
Of the sweets of Faeries, Peris, Goddesses,
There is not such a treat among them all,
Haunters of cavern, lake, and waterfall,
As a real woman, lineal indeed
From Pyrrha's pebbles or old Adam's seed.
Thus gentle Lamia judg'd, and judg'd aright,
That Lycius could not love in half a fright,
So threw the goddess off, and won his heart
More pleasantly by playing woman's part,
With no more awe than what her beauty gave,
That, while it smote, still guaranteed to save.

Lycius to all made eloquent reply,
Marrying to every word a twinborn sigh;
And last, pointing to Corinth, ask'd her sweet,
If 'twas too far that night for her soft feet.
The way was short, for Lamia's eagerness
Made, by a spell, the triple league decrease
To a few paces; not at all surmised
By blinded Lycius, so in her comprized.
They pass'd the city gates, he knew not how
So noiseless, and he never thought to know.

As men talk in a dream, so Corinth all,
Throughout her palaces imperial,
And all her populous streets and temples lewd,
Mutter'd, like tempest in the distance brew'd,
To the wide-spreaded night above her towers.
Men, women, rich and poor, in the cool hours,
Shuffled their sandals o'er the pavement white,
Companion'd or alone; while many a light
Flared, here and there, from wealthy festivals,
And threw their moving shadows on the walls,
Or found them cluster'd in the corniced shade
Of some arch'd temple door, or dusky colonnade.

Muffling his face, of greeting friends in fear,
Her fingers he press'd hard, as one came near
With curl'd gray beard, sharp eyes, and smooth bald crown,
Slow-stepp'd, and robed in philosophic gown:
Lycius shrank closer, as they met and past,
Into his mantle, adding wings to haste,
While hurried Lamia trembled: 'Ah,' said he,
Why do you shudder, love, so ruefully?
Why does your tender palm dissolve in dew?'–
'I'm wearied,' said fair Lamia: 'tell me who
Is that old man? I cannot bring to mind

His features – Lycius! wherefore did you blind
Yourself from his quick eyes?' Lycius replied,
''Tis Apollonius sage, my trusty guide
And good instructor; but to-night he seems
The ghost of folly haunting my sweet dreams.'

While yet he spake they had arrived before
A pillar'd porch, with lofty portal door,
Where hung a silver lamp, whose phosphor glow
Reflected in the slabbed steps below,
Mild as a star in water; for so new,
And so unsullied was the marble's hue,
So through the crystal polish, liquid fine,
Ran the dark veins, that none but feet divine
Could e'er have touch'd there. Sounds Aeolian
Breath'd from the hinges, as the ample span
Of the wide doors disclos'd a place unknown
Some time to any, but those two alone,
And a few Persian mutes, who that same year
Were seen about the markets: none knew where
They could inhabit; the most curious
Were foil'd, who watch'd to trace them to their house:
And but the flitter-winged verse must tell,
For truth's sake, what woe afterwards befel,
'Twould humour many a heart to leave them thus,
Shut from the busy world of more incredulous.

PART II

Love in a hut, with water and a crust,
Is – Love, forgive us! – cinders, ashes, dust;
Love in a palace is perhaps at last
More grievous torment than a hermit's fast: –
That is a doubtful tale from faery land,

Hard for the non-elect to understand.
Had Lycius liv'd to hand his story down,
He might have given the moral a fresh frown,
Or clench'd it quite: but too short was their bliss
To breed distrust and hate, that make the soft voice hiss.
Besides, there, nightly, with terrific glare,
Love, jealous grown of so complete a pair,
Hover'd and buzz'd his wings, with fearful roar,
Above the lintel of their chamber door,
And down the passage cast a glow upon the floor.

For all this came a ruin: side by side
They were enthroned, in the even tide,
Upon a couch, near to a curtaining
Whose airy texture, from a golden string,
Floated into the room, and let appear
Unveil'd the summer heaven, blue and clear,
Betwixt two marble shafts:– there they reposed,
Where use had made it sweet, with eyelids closed,
Saving a tythe which love still open kept,
That they might see each other while they almost slept;
When from the slope side of a suburb hill,
Deafening the swallow's twitter, came a thrill
Of trumpets – Lycius started – the sounds fled,
But left a thought, a buzzing in his head.
For the first time, since first he harbour'd in
That purple-lined palace of sweet sin,
His spirit pass'd beyond its golden bourn
Into the noisy world almost forsworn.
The lady, ever watchful, penetrant,
Saw this with pain, so arguing a want
Of something more, more than her empery
Of joys; and she began to moan and sigh
Because he mused beyond her, knowing well
That but a moment's thought is passion's passing bell.

'Why do you sigh, fair creature?' whisper'd he:
'Why do you think?' return'd she tenderly:
'You have deserted me – where am I now?
Not in your heart while care weighs on your brow:
No, no, you have dismiss'd me; and I go
From your breast houseless: ay, it must be so.'
He answer'd, bending to her open eyes,
Where he was mirror'd small in paradise,
'My silver planet, both of eve and morn!
Why will you plead yourself so sad forlorn,
While I am striving how to fill my heart
With deeper crimson, and a double smart?
How to entangle, trammel up and snare
Your soul in mine, and labyrinth you there
Like the hid scent in an unbudded rose?
Aye, a sweet kiss – you see your mighty woes.
My thoughts! shall I unveil them? Listen then!
What mortal hath a prize, that other men
May be confounded and abash'd withal,
But lets it sometimes pace abroad majestical,
And triumph, as in thee I should rejoice
Amid the hoarse alarm of Corinth's voice.
Let my foes choke, and my friends shout afar,
While through the thronged streets your bridal car
Wheels round its dazzling spokes.' – The lady's cheek
Trembled; she nothing said, but, pale and meek,
Arose and knelt before him, wept a rain
Of sorrows at his words; at last with pain
Beseeching him, the while his hand she wrung,
To change his purpose. He thereat was stung,
Perverse, with stronger fancy to reclaim
Her wild and timid nature to his aim:
Besides, for all his love, in self despite,
Against his better self, he took delight
Luxurious in her sorrows, soft and new.

His passion, cruel grown, took on a hue
Fierce and sanguineous as 'twas possible
In one whose brow had no dark veins to swell.
Fine was the mitigated fury, like
Apollo's presence when in act to strike
The serpent – Ha, the serpent! certes, she
Was none. She burnt, she lov'd the tyranny,
And, all subdued, consented to the hour
When to the bridal he should lead his paramour.
Whispering in midnight silence, said the youth,
'Sure some sweet name thou hast, though, by my truth,
I have not ask'd it, ever thinking thee
Not mortal, but of heavenly progeny,
As still I do. Hast any mortal name,
Fit appellation for this dazzling frame?
Or friends or kinsfolk on the citied earth,
To share our marriage feast and nuptial mirth?'
'I have no friends,' said Lamia, 'no, not one;
My presence in wide Corinth hardly known:
My parents' bones are in their dusty urns
Sepulchred, where no kindled incense burns,
Seeing all their luckless race are dead, save me,
And I neglect the holy rite for thee.
Even as you list invite your many guests;
But if, as now it seems, your vision rests
With any pleasure on me, do not bid
Old Apollonius – from him keep me hid.'
Lycius, perplex'd at words so blind and blank,
Made close inquiry; from whose touch she shrank,
Feigning a sleep; and he to the dull shade
Of deep sleep in a moment was betray'd.

It was the custom then to bring away
The bride from home at blushing shut of day,
Veil'd, in a chariot, heralded along

By strewn flowers, torches, and a marriage song,
With other pageants: but this fair unknown
Had not a friend. So being left alone,
 (Lycius was gone to summon all his kin)
And knowing surely she could never win
His foolish heart from its mad pompousness,
She set herself, high-thoughted, how to dress
The misery in fit magnificence.
She did so, but 'tis doubtful how and whence
Came, and who were her subtle servitors.
About the halls, and to and from the doors,
There was a noise of wings, till in short space
The glowing banquet-room shone with wide-arched grace.
A haunting music, sole perhaps and lone
Supportress of the faery-roof, made moan
Throughout, as fearful the whole charm might fade.
Fresh carved cedar, mimicking a glade
Of palm and plantain, met from either side,
High in the midst, in honour of the bride:
Two palms and then two plantains, and so on,
From either side their stems branch'd one to one
All down the aisled place; and beneath all
There ran a stream of lamps straight on from wall to wall.
So canopied, lay an untasted feast
Teeming with odours. Lamia, regal drest,
Silently paced about, and as she went,
In pale contented sort of discontent,
Mission'd her viewless servants to enrich
The fretted splendour of each nook and niche.
Between the tree-stems, marbled plain at first,
Came jasper pannels; then, anon, there burst
Forth creeping imagery of slighter trees,
And with the larger wove in small intricacies.
Approving all, she faded at self-will,
And shut the chamber up, close, hush'd and still,

Complete and ready for the revels rude,
When dreadful guests would come to spoil her solitude.

The day appear'd, and all the gossip rout.
O senseless Lycius! Madman! wherefore flout
The silent-blessing fate, warm cloister'd hours,
And show to common eyes these secret bowers?
The herd approach'd; each guest, with busy brain,
Arriving at the portal, gaz'd amain,
And enter'd marveling: for they knew the street,
Remember'd it from childhood all complete
Without a gap, yet ne'er before had seen
That royal porch, that high-built fair demesne;
So in they hurried all, maz'd, curious and keen:
Save one, who look'd thereon with eye severe,
And with calm-planted steps walk'd in austere;
'Twas Apollonius: something too he laugh'd,
As though some knotty problem, that had daft
His patient thought, had now begun to thaw,
And solve and melt – 'twas just as he foresaw.

He met within the murmurous vestibule
His young disciple. ''Tis no common rule,
Lycius,' said he, 'for uninvited guest
To force himself upon you, and infest
With an unbidden presence the bright throng
Of younger friends; yet must I do this wrong,
And you forgive me.' Lycius blush'd, and led
The old man through the inner doors broad-spread;
With reconciling words and courteous mien
Turning into sweet milk the sophist's spleen.

Of wealthy lustre was the banquet-room,
Fill'd with pervading brilliance and perfume:
Before each lucid pannel fuming stood

A censer fed with myrrh and spiced wood,
Each by a sacred tripod held aloft,
Whose slender feet wide-swerv'd upon the soft
Wool-woofed carpets: fifty wreaths of smoke
From fifty censers their light voyage took
To the high roof, still mimick'd as they rose
Along the mirror'd walls by twin-clouds odorous.
Twelve sphered tables, by silk seats insphered,
High as the level of a man's breast rear'd
On libbard's paws, upheld the heavy gold
Of cups and goblets, and the store thrice told
Of Ceres' horn, and, in huge vessels, wine
Come from the gloomy tun with merry shine.
Thus loaded with a feast the tables stood,
Each shrining in the midst the image of a God.

When in an antichamber every guest
Had felt the cold full sponge to pleasure press'd,
By minist'ring slaves, upon his hands and feet,
And fragrant oils with ceremony meet
Pour'd on his hair, they all mov'd to the feast
In white robes, and themselves in order placed
Around the silken couches, wondering
Whence all this mighty cost and blaze of wealth could spring.

Soft went the music the soft air along,
While fluent Greek a vowel'd undersong
Kept up among the guests discoursing low
At first, for scarcely was the wine at flow;
But when the happy vintage touch'd their brains,
Louder they talk, and louder come the strains
Of powerful instruments: – the gorgeous dyes,
The space, the splendour of the draperies,
The roof of awful richness, nectarous cheer,
Beautiful slaves, and Lamia's self, appear,

Now, when the wine has done its rosy deed,
And every soul from human trammels freed,
No more so strange; for merry wine, sweet wine,
Will make Elysian shades not too fair, too divine.
Soon was God Bacchus at meridian height;
Flush'd were their cheeks, and bright eyes double bright:
Garlands of every green, and every scent
From vales deflower'd, or forest-trees branch-rent,
In baskets of bright osier'd gold were brought
High as the handles heap'd, to suit the thought
Of every guest; that each, as he did please,
Might fancy-fit his brows, silk-pillow'd at his ease.

What wreath for Lamia? What for Lycius?
What for the sage, old Apollonius?
Upon her aching forehead be there hung
The leaves of willow and of adder's tongue;
And for the youth, quick, let us strip for him
The thyrsus, that his watching eyes may swim
Into forgetfulness; and, for the sage,
Let spear-grass and the spiteful thistle wage
War on his temples. Do not all charms fly
At the mere touch of cold philosophy?
There was an awful rainbow once in heaven:
We know her woof, her texture; she is given
In the dull catalogue of common things.
Philosophy will clip an Angel's wings,
Conquer all mysteries by rule and line,
Empty the haunted air, and gnomed mine –
Unweave a rainbow, as it erewhile made
The tender-person'd Lamia melt into a shade.
By her glad Lycius sitting, in chief place,
Scarce saw in all the room another face,
Till, checking his love trance, a cup he took
Full brimm'd, and opposite sent forth a look

'Cross the broad table, to beseech a glance
From his old teacher's wrinkled countenance,
And pledge him. The bald-head philosopher
Had fix'd his eye, without a twinkle or stir
Full on the alarmed beauty of the bride,
Brow-beating her fair form, and troubling her sweet pride.
Lycius then press'd her hand, with devout touch,
As pale it lay upon the rosy couch:
'Twas icy, and the cold ran through his veins;
Then sudden it grew hot, and all the pains
Of an unnatural heat shot to his heart.
'Lamia, what means this? Wherefore dost thou start?
Know'st thou that man?' Poor Lamia answer'd not.
He gaz'd into her eyes, and not a jot
Own'd they the lovelorn piteous appeal:
More, more he gaz'd: his human senses reel:
Some hungry spell that loveliness absorbs;
There was no recognition in those orbs.
'Lamia!' he cried – and no soft-toned reply.
The many heard, and the loud revelry
Grew hush; the stately music no more breathes;
The myrtle sicken'd in a thousand wreaths.
By faint degrees, voice, lute, and pleasure ceased;
A deadly silence step by step increased,
Until it seem'd a horrid presence there,
And not a man but felt the terror in his hair.
'Lamia!' he shriek'd; and nothing but the shriek
With its sad echo did the silence break.
'Begone, foul dream!' he cried, gazing again
In the bride's face, where now no azure vein
Wander'd on fair-spaced temples; no soft bloom
Misted the cheek; no passion to illume
The deep-recessed vision: –all was blight;
Lamia, no longer fair, there sat a deadly white.
'Shut, shut those juggling eyes, thou ruthless man!

Turn them aside, wretch! or the righteous ban
Of all the Gods, whose dreadful images
Here represent their shadowy presences,
May pierce them on the sudden with the thorn
Of painful blindness; leaving thee forlorn,
In trembling dotage to the feeblest fright
Of conscience, for their long offended might,
For all thine impious proud-heart sophistries,
Unlawful magic, and enticing lies.
Corinthians! look upon that gray-beard wretch!
Mark how, possess'd, his lashless eyelids stretch
Around his demon eyes! Corinthians, see!
My sweet bride withers at their potency.'
'Fool!' said the sophist, in an under-tone
Gruff with contempt; which a death-nighing moan
From Lycius answer'd, as heart-struck and lost,
He sank supine beside the aching ghost.
'Fool! Fool!' repeated he, while his eyes still
Relented not, nor mov'd; 'from every ill
Of life have I preserv'd thee to this day,
And shall I see thee made a serpent's prey?'
Then Lamia breath'd death breath; the sophist's eye,
Like a sharp spear, went through her utterly,
Keen, cruel, perceant, stinging: she, as well
As her weak hand could any meaning tell,
Motion'd him to be silent; vainly so,
He look'd and look'd again a level – No!
'A Serpent!' echoed he; no sooner said,
Than with a frightful scream she vanished:
And Lycius' arms were empty of delight,
As were his limbs of life, from that same night.
On the high couch he lay! – his friends came round –
Supported him – no pulse, or breath they found,
And, in its marriage robe, the heavy body wound.

Money was much on Keats's mind that summer as his finances became desperate. He attempted to call in his numerous debts among his circle of friends, with scant success. In May he appears to have even considered returning to medicine, and becoming a ship's surgeon journeying to and from India for a few years. At the end of the summer he resolved to try journalism for a more regular income that would allow him to write. Both ideas came to nothing, but indicate the extent of his desperation, and a sense of crisis and finality in his circumstances. Envious of Byron's commercial success with John Murray he even momentarily considered changing publishers, offering his new poems to the man who had set his critic on Keats in *The Quarterly*. (He wisely stayed with Taylor and Hessey, whose relationship with Keats went beyond the professional, supporting him financially on his doomed trip to Italy and never losing faith in his poetic potential.) And he collaborated with Brown on a speculative play-script during their time together at Shanklin. *Otho the Great* was expressly calculated to bring in ready money, its authors hoping they could convince Edmund Kean, the foremost Shakespearean actor of the day, to stage their play at Drury Lane. Brown supplied the incidents, and Keats worked it up into verse drama, labouring on it diligently throughout July and August. To little effect. They shortly learned that Kean proposed to tour America, whilst the play itself is wooden and bombastic and of little credit to Keats's reputation. The year of wonder, which started so triumphantly, threatened to peter out. Until Autumn.

Keats had become thoroughly disenchanted with the Isle of Wight, and needed a change of scene, as well as a library for researching 'Lamia'. He chose Winchester, and travelled there on 12th August. The weather was again glorious, something that appeared to affect his temperament and outlook profoundly. He wrote to his sister at the end of August how 'The delightful Weather we have had for two Months is the highest gratification I could receive – no chill'd red noses – no shivering

– but fair Atmosphere to think in... I adore fine Weather as the greatest blessing I can have.' It meant health, outdoors, expansive blue skies under which he could experience nature at its finest and fullest. As he did on the walk he took on Sunday 19th September 1819. This walk resulted in his final Great Ode. 'To Autumn', one of his last completed poems, is the summation of that fruitful year, both high point and end point of a genius fulfilled.

To Autumn

I

Season of mist and mellow fruitfulness,
*   Close bosom-friend of the maturing sun;*
Conspiring with him how to load and bless
*   With fruit the vines that round the thatch-eves run;*
To bend with apples the moss'd cottage-trees,
*   And fill all fruit with ripeness to the core;*
*   To swell the gourd, and plump the hazel shells*
*   With a sweet kernel; to set budding more,*
And still more, later flowers for the bees,
Until they think warm days will never cease,
*   For Summer has o'er-brimmed their clammy cells.*

II

Who hath not seen thee oft amid thy store?
*   Sometimes whoever seeks abroad may find*
Thee sitting careless on a granary floor,
*   Thy hair soft-lifted by the winnowing wind;*
Or on a half-reap'd furrow sound asleep,
*   Drows'd with the fume of poppies, while thy hook*
*   Spares the next swath and all its twined flowers:*
And sometimes like a gleaner thou dost keep

Steady thy laden head across the brook;
Or by a cyder-press, with patient look,
   Thou watchest the last oozings hours by hours.

III

Where are the songs of Spring? Ay, where are they?
  Think not of them, thou hast thy music too, –
While barred clouds bloom the soft-dying day,
 And touch the stubble-plains with rosy hue;
Then in wailful choir the small gnats mourn
  Among the river sallows, borne aloft
   Or sinking as the light wind lives or dies;
And full-grown lambs loud bleat from hilly bourn;
  Hedge-crickets sing; and now with treble soft
  The red-breast whistles from a garden-croft;
   And gathering swallows twitter in the skies.

Keats was never really a 'nature' poet. The bowers, brooks and budding sweets of his early poems are the decorative fantasies of a born and bred Londoner who had gorged himself on Classical fable. The landscape of 'Grecian Urn' was two-dimensional and transcendent, that of 'Nightingale' a vague, twilit stage set for the dialogue between symbol and soul. In 'Autumn' Keats comes closest to evoking and engaging with a recognisable, albeit idealised, pastoral world in itself. The 'I' of 'Psyche' and 'Nightingale' retreats, replaced by the recording 'eye' that captures the scene in slow time. All the senses, in fact, are put to work harvesting the full experience of a world enriched by the season. Touch in the first stanza, with the warmth of the maturing sun, and the clamminess of its golden store; sight in the second, as both poet and Autumn personified watch patiently the slow-garnering of its bounty; and sound in the final, as nature strikes up its elegy to the dying year.

As with the walk that occasioned it, the poem progresses from the enclosed domesticity of a cottage garden, to the wider world of agriculture, and the even wider world, with the migrating birds departing as the globe turns away from the sun. The progression is temporal as well as spatial: from the misty start of a late-summer morning in the first stanza, to the dying breath of early evening and approaching winter in the last. The middle stanza, the middle line in fact, stands in perfect equipoise, with its image of Autumn personified: 'Drowsed with the fume of poppies, while thy hook / Spares the next swath and all its twined flowers'. Time, the antagonist whom Keats kept at bay in 'Grecian Urn' by the escapist artifice of its eternal spring, is stilled here in a moment of natural serenity, poised at a threshold. A momentary truce with Time, achieved through acceptance, rather than escapism. The season, the earth, the poet stand fleetingly still – his immortality assured as poetry comes as close as it can to perfection… Then the earth turns slowly once more, away from the sun that gives it life, and Time picks up his scythe. Ripeness is all.

Winter

It is difficult in retrospect not to read 'Autumn' as Keats's swan-song, a final, definitive, maybe even part-conscious statement of completion. As Keats had stated in his earlier allegory of human life, 'The Human Seasons':

> ... *quiet coves*
> *His soul has in its Autumn, when his wings*
>   *He furleth close; contented so to look*
> *On mists in idleness – to let fair things*
>   *Pass by unheeded as a threshold brook.*

As summer relinquishes its hold on the year replete with perfection, so the poet, having scaled the heights, finally furls his wings. The tormented questor of the spring Odes gives way to the serene observer of a warm, living and ultimately dying pastoral. Shelley ends his turbulent autumnal ode 'To the West Wind' with the optimistic reflection, 'If Winter comes, can Spring be far behind?'. Keats's poem ends with finality; all thoughts of spring and its songs banished with the departing swallows. Exactly a year later Keats would follow those birds south, but in truth departing for that other, 'undiscovered country' from which no traveller returns.

Keats returned from Winchester to London in early October 1819. Not to Hampstead, but to rooms in Westminster, to set up as a journalist. He had written to Brown on 22nd September (three days after writing 'Autumn') declaring:

> It is quite time I should set myself doing something, and live no longer upon hopes. … I will write, on the liberal side of the question, for whoever will pay me. I have not known yet what it is to be diligent. I purpose living in town in a cheap lodging, and endeavouring, for a beginning, to get the theatricals of some paper…

This finds Keats as resolute as he has been for a good long time. 'Purpose' is not a term we might readily associate with the Keats of summer 1819. In the late spring he had professed to a mood of 'indolence', and composed an Ode on it.

Ode on Indolence
'They toil not, neither do they spin.'

I

One morn before me were three figures seen,
*   With bowed necks, and joined hands, side-faced;*
And one behind the other stepp'd serene,
*   In placid sandals, and in white robes graced;*
They pass'd, like figures on a marble urn,
*   When shifted round to see the other side;*
*   They came again; as when the urn once more*
Is shifted round, the first seen shades return;
*   And they were strange to me, as may betide*
*   With vases, to one deep in Phidian lore.*

II

How is it, Shadows! that I knew ye not?
*   How came ye muffled in so hush a mask?*

Was it a silent deep-disguised plot
    To steal away, and leave without a task
My idle days? Ripe was the drowsy hour;
    The blissful cloud of summer-indolence
        Benumb'd my eyes; my pulse grew less and less;
Pain had no sting, and pleasure's wreath no flower:
    O, why did ye not melt, and leave my sense
        Unhaunted quite of all but – nothingness?

III

A third time pass'd they by, and, passing, turn'd
    Each one the face a moment whiles to me;
Then faded, and to follow them I burn'd
    And ach'd for wings because I knew the three;
The first was a fair Maid, and Love her name;
    The second was Ambition, pale of cheek,
        And ever watchful with fatigued eye;
The last, whom I love more, the more of blame
    Is heap'd upon her, maiden most unmeek, –
        I knew to be my demon Poesy.

IV

They faded, and, forsooth! I wanted wings:
    O folly! What is love! and where is it?
And for that poor Ambition! it springs
    From a man's little heart's short fever-fit;
For Poesy! – no, – she has not a joy, –
    At least for me, – so sweet as drowsy noons,
        And evenings steep'd in honied indolence;
O, for an age so shelter'd from annoy,
    That I may never know how change the moons,
        Or hear the voice of busy common-sense!

V

And once more came they by; – alas! wherefore?
My sleep had been embroider'd with dim dreams;
My soul had been a lawn besprinkled o'er
With flowers, and stirring shades, and baffled beams:
The morn was clouded, but no shower fell,
Tho' in her lids hung the sweet tears of May;
The open casement press'd a new-leav'd vine,
Let in the budding warmth and throstle's lay;
O Shadows! 'twas a time to bid farewell!
Upon your skirts had fallen no tears of mine.

VI

So, ye three Ghosts, adieu! Ye cannot raise
My head cool-bedded in the flowery grass;
For I would not be dieted with praise,
A pet-lamb in a sentimental farce!
Fade softly from my eyes, and be once more
In masque-like figures on the dreamy urn;
Farewell! I yet have visions for the night,
And for the day faint visions there is store;
Vanish, ye Phantoms! from my idle spright,
Into the clouds, and never more return!

Yet the voice of busy common sense cannot be ignored for ever. Warm days do finally cease and every summer holiday comes to an end. It is thus that we find Keats returning to London resolved to do 'something', shake off idleness and false hopes and buckle down to earning his crust. This more practical scheme would, he reasoned, allow him 'to compose deliberate poems' when he could afford to.

Keats chose Westminster ostensibly to be close to the political world for writing on the liberal side of debates, and closer to the

West End theatres for his reviews. Yet it also kept him at arm's length from Fanny, who was evidently one conflict the summer or his verse sophistries had failed to resolve. He told Brown, 'I like —————— [Miss Brawne] and cannot help it. On that account I had better not live there [Hampstead].' Still the secrecy, still the evasion, the tortured paradox of the poet who fears 'happiness', and runs from the thing he loves. The newly resolute and practical Keats still clung to his emotional independence.

Keats rarely knew his own mind. According to his publisher Hessey, he 'is such a man of fits and starts, he is not much to be depended on'. Never more so than in the swift change that came over the scorner of domestic happiness on his return to London that autumn. He visited Fanny on 10th October, and there immediately followed a string of ardent letters (almost as many as he had written all summer). In the first he declared himself 'dazzled' by her, at 'her mercy', but no longer resisting the tender yoke of love. Two days later he writes her that he can think of nothing else, and that 'The time is passed when I had power to advise and warn you [against] the unpromising morning of my Life – My Love has made me selfish. I cannot exist without you.' He had once said the same of poetry, writing to Reynolds in April 1817, how 'I find that I cannot exist without poetry... half the day will not do.' Now it is Fanny he must have. The erstwhile apostle of an 'abstract Beauty' now declares that 'Love is my Religion – I could die for that – I could die for you. My Creed is Love and you are its only tenet.' A week later he moves back to Hampstead, telling Fanny how he 'must impose chains upon' himself, must clip his independent wings. Icarus, dazzled by his bright star, finally falls to earth.

Keats's plan to live as a journalist produced not a line. His determination to live no longer on false hopes melted like snow. On his return to Hampstead the couple made firm their emotional commitment in a secret engagement, whatever the material consequences. He knew his devotion to Fanny was 'selfish', for his prospects were no better, indeed a good deal worse, than they had been when they first met a year before. There were glimmerings of hope late in the year, when Tom's part of the inheritance was freed from legal wrangles, enabling Keats to settle his numerous debts. But it also effectively allowed George to carry off most of the pot back to America. Keats was open-hearted, open-handed and completely impractical. He once claimed that 'George always stood between me and any dealings with the world.' George, now married, with one child and another on the way, struggling to survive in an alien land, had his own interests to pursue. Desperation forced George to cross the Atlantic as the old year ended, and he took about £700 (an enormous sum), leaving Keats effectively penniless once again. As Keats mused to Brown, 'that was not fair, was it?'. The two brothers parted at the end of January for the very last time, and the regular correspondence between them became a thing of the past.

The creativity that had blossomed so extraordinarily in that year of wonder also deserted him towards the end. 'The Cap and Bells', the final long poem he attempted, and his last sustained effort at writing verse, occupied him for most of November and December 1819. This was something of a departure for Keats, giving full vent to the more Byronic satirical voice that had crept into 'Lamia' in places. Its principal target has been identified as the Prince Regent, soon-to-be George IV, and his corrupt sycophantic court. But it also swipes at the contemporary literary world Keats had failed to conquer. Its alternative title, appropriately enough, is 'The Jealousies'.

Keats had been viewing the literary world he had launched himself into so passionately and hopefully with a rueful irony for some time. In the spring, between his Odes 'to Psyche' and 'On a Grecian Urn', he had written a sonnet 'On Fame'.

> *Fame, like a wayward Girl, will still be coy*
> *   To those who woo her with too slavish knees,*
> *But makes surrender to some thoughtless Boy,*

> *And dotes the more upon a heart at ease;*
> *She is a Gipsey, will not speak to those*
> > *Who have not learnt to be content without her;*
> *A Jilt, whose ear was never whisper'd close,*
> > *Who thinks they scandal her who talk about her;*
> *A very Gipsey is she, Nilus-born,*
> > *Sister-in-law to jealous Potiphar:*
> *Ye love-sick Bards, repay her scorn for scorn,*
> > *Ye Artists lovelorn, madmen that ye are!*
> *Make your best bow to her and bid adieu,*
> *Then if she likes it, she will follow you.*

Keats was certainly making his best bow at that time, rejecting the 'gipsy' fame at the very moment he was producing the poems that would eventually secure her. He had planned to publish 'The Cap and Bells' under a pseudonym, and had used one for 'La Belle Dame Sans Merci', when it appeared in Hunt's *The Indicator* in May 1820. The name he would come to claim was writ in water, he was already starting to erase. In December Keats abandoned 'The Cap and Bells'. Like so many of the long poems he had tried before, it ends in mid sentence. His best bow made in the works that would make him immortal, it but remained for him to make his awkward bow to the world and leave the stage.

The beginning of the end happened on 4th February 1820, a few days after George set off back to America, and the brothers parted for the very last time. Keats had ventured into central London, making the most of a mild day in a deep-frozen winter to attend to some business. He may have spent longer in town than he had intended, and returned to Hampstead after dark, without his new winter coat, travelling as usual on the outside of the coach. According to Brown, Keats arrived at Wentworth Place fevered and weak, and he sent him straight to bed. When Brown came up with some spirits to revive him, Keats was just climbing into bed. As he did so he coughed, tasted blood in his mouth, and asked for a candle to confirm his fears. A single spot had fallen on the cold white sheet. Brown records the rest: 'After regarding it steadfastly, he looked up in my face, with a calmness of countenance that I can never forget, and said, "I know the colour of that blood; – it is arterial blood; – I cannot be deceived in that colour; – that drop of blood is my death warrant; – I must die."' A much larger haemorrhage from his lungs followed shortly, which 'nearly suffocated' Keats. Something that would become a regular occurrence over the twelve months that were now left to him.

Keats was trained in medicine. He had nursed his mother and then his brother through all the stages of the disease that now appeared to be clearly manifest in himself. He was surely right to be so certain. Yet, even to the last, not until his body was opened up to find his lungs quite destroyed by the disease, his doctor in Rome would not accept what we might assume was inevitable, predestined or foreknown by the poet. Did Keats really know this, as Brown's anecdote suggests? Did he also believe his early death inevitable, confirmed in this apparently definitive moment?

Samuel Taylor Coleridge claims he knew Keats was marked out for an early grave on the brief meeting he had with him back in the fine spring of 1819. Coleridge was out walking on Hampstead Heath, near his Highgate home, with a medical friend whom Keats had known at Guy's Hospital in London. Keats shook the older poet's hand, and as he walked away, Coleridge claims to have remarked, 'There was death in that hand.' We can't read Keats's hand, but we can read the works of those hands, some of which urge us to contemplate these very questions. Just a few months before Keats beheld his 'death warrant' in that drop of blood he scribbled the following lines on the manuscript of 'The Cap and Bells':

This living hand, now warm and capable,
Or earnest grasping, would, if it were cold
And in the icy silence of the tomb,
So haunt thy days and chill thy dreaming nights

That thou wouldst wish thine own heart dry of blood
So in my veins red life might stream again,
And thou be conscience-calm'd – see here it is –
I hold it towards you.

The appeal unnerves with its directness, haunting us indeed with its pathos and chill foreboding of what would shortly ensue. This gesture evidently spoke feelingly for Keats, as he had used it earlier in the opening lines of *The Fall of Hyperion* (the abortive revision of his epic):

Fanatics have their dreams, wherewith they weave
A paradise for a sect; the savage too
From forth the loftiest fashion of his sleep
Guesses at Heaven; pity these have not
Trac'd upon the vellum or wild Indian leaf
The shadows of melodious utterance.
But bare of laurel they live, dream, and die;
For Poesy alone can tell her dreams,
With the fine spell of words alone can save
Imagination from the sable chain
And dumb enchantment. Who alive can say,
'Thou art no Poet – may'st not tell thy dreams?'
Since every man whose soul is not a clod
Hath visions, and would speak, if he had loved,
And been well nurtured in his mother tongue.
Whether the dream now purpos'd to rehearse
Be poet's or fanatic's will be known
When this warm scribe my hand is in the grave.

These lines also speak from beyond the grave, directly addressing posterity (us in fact) to assess his achievement. Only time could tell, and time was running out.

And yet, Keats had ever betrayed an acute sense of being up against time. In 'Sleep and Poetry' he had asked 'for ten years, that I may / Overwhelm myself in poesy', displaying an urgent honesty, but also anxiety in the eighteen-year-old aspirant poet. The anxiety is best summed up in Keats's sonnet, 'When I have fears that I may cease to be' (December 1818). Keats's ambition was huge, but his likely allocation of life short. This realisation drove him on when he felt optimistic, spurring him (prematurely) into epic ventures; but also inwards and downwards when he acknowledged that time might just be against him:

> When I have fears that I may cease to be
>   Before my pen has glean'd my teeming brain,
> Before high-piled books, in charactery,
>   Hold like rich garners the full ripen'd grain;
> When I behold, upon the night's starr'd face,
>   Huge cloudy symbols of a high romance,
> And think that I may never live to trace
>   Their shadows, with the magic hand of chance;
> And when I feel, fair creature of an hour,
>   That I shall never look upon thee more,
> Never have relish in the faery power
>   Of unreflecting love; – then on the shore
> Of the wide world I stand alone, and think
> Till love and fame to nothingness do sink.

Sinking into nothingness, his name as ephemeral as the waves washing the shore, was his final despairing desire, anticipated in the dying fall of this and so many endings in his verse. Such an early poem, 'After Dark Vapours' (January 1817), concludes with a tumbling string of associations leading by some inexorable logic to the foreboding final image:

> After dark vapors have oppress'd our plains
>   For a long dreary season, comes a day
>   Born of the gentle South, and clears away
> From the sick heavens all unseemly stains.

> *The anxious month, relieved of all its pains,*
> > *Takes as a long-lost right the feel of May;*
> > *The eyelids with the passing coolness play*
> *Like rose leaves with the drip of Summer rains.*
> *The calmest thoughts come round us; as of leaves*
> > *Budding – fruit ripening in stillness – Autumn suns*
> *Smiling at eve upon the quiet sheaves –*
> *Sweet Sappho's cheek – a smiling infant's breath –*
> > *The gradual sand that through an hour-glass runs –*
> *A woodland rivulet – a Poet's death.*

And when the reviewers had snatched hope from his warm living hands, it was the idea of posthumous fame that consoled Keats, for he declared defiantly to his brother that he would be among the English poets *after his death*.

Death's shadow fell starkly across the verse monument Keats was etching. If such preoccupations compelled him to spend his short life attempting long poems, they also encouraged the big themes of his shorter lyrics. Mortality is ever the concern of the immortals. Of Shakespeare's sonnets, like Keats, obsessed with the human seasons,

> *That time of year thou mayst in me behold*
> *When yellow leaves, or none, or few, do hang*
> *Upon those boughs which shake against the cold,*
> *Bare ruin'd choirs, where late the sweet birds sang.*
> – Sonnet 73

Of Donne and Marvell; Hardy, MacNeice or Auden. Keats's early death and his anxious anticipations of it may have contributed to his myth, but they also shaped and secured his immortality in verse.

Eighteen-hundred-and-nineteen had found Keats at his most troubled and confused. Debt, desire and ambition had incessantly pulled him in conflicting directions. Illness simplified his options: he would live or die. But he would also love, and he clung to Fanny as his final hope for happiness this side of the grave. Keats may have composed his most famous and best poem inspired by Fanny at this period (its exact date is highly conjectural). If not written at this time, its sentiments do accord with those expressed in his letters, of a poet newly 'dazzled' by the beauty of a beloved, and dedicating himself to his new creed:

Bright-Star! would I were steadfast as thou art

Bright star, would I were stedfast as thou art –
  Not in lone splendour hung aloft the night
And watching, with eternal lids apart,
  Like nature's patient, sleepless Eremite,
The moving waters at their priestlike task
  Of pure ablution round earth's human shores,
Or gazing on the new soft-fallen mask
  Of snow upon the mountains and the moors –
No – yet still stedfast, still unchangeable,
  Pillow'd upon my fair love's ripening breast,
To feel for ever its soft fall and swell,
  Awake for ever in a sweet unrest
Still, still to hear her tender-taken breath,
And so live ever – or else swoon to death.

The final line, with its customary glance at the 'fell sergeant' Death, is perhaps given a more urgent poignancy now he had made his choice to love.

Keats clung to Fanny as devotedly as he had once clung to his ambitions. In many ways the 'minx' Fanny replaced the 'gipsy' Fame, and troubled him as sorely with the ardency of his impossible love. His poem 'To Fanny', written shortly after his first haemorrhage in February 1820, describes his 'torturing jealousies'. The unsure, wandering Keats, who had kept his distance because of his doubts or scruples, is now confined to his sick-room, and resents his young love's mobility. It is his turn to imprison, jealously demanding that Fanny curbs her flirtatious wanderings.

To Fanny

I

Physician Nature! let my spirit blood!
  O ease my heart of verse and let me rest;
Throw me upon thy Tripod, till the flood
  Of stifling numbers ebbs from my full breast.
A theme! a theme! great nature! give a theme;
    Let me begin my dream.
I come – I see thee, as thou standest there,
Beckon me not into the wintery air.

II

Ah! dearest love, sweet home of all my fears,
  And hopes and joys, and panting miseries, –
To-night, if I may guess, thy beauty wears
    A smile of such delight,
    As brilliant and as bright,
As when with ravished, aching, vassal eyes,
    Lost in soft amaze,
    I gaze, I gaze!

III

Who now, with greedy looks, eats up my feast?
  What stare outfaces now my silver moon!
Ah! keep that hand unravished at the least;

Let, let, the amorous burn –
But, pr'ythee, do not turn
The current of your heart from me so soon.
O! save, in charity,
The quickest pulse for me.

Save it for me, sweet love! though music breathe
Voluptuous visions into the warm air;
Though swimming through the dance's dangerous wreath,
Be like an April day,
Smiling and cold and gay,
A temperate lilly, temperate as fair;
Then, Heaven! there will be
A warmer June for me.

Why, this – you'll say, my Fanny! is not true:
Put your soft hand upon your snowy side,
Where the heart beats: confess – 'tis nothing new –
Must not a woman be
A feather on the sea,
Sway'd to and fro by every wind and tide?
Of as uncertain speed
As blow-ball from the mead?

I know it – and to know it is despair
To one who loves you as I love, sweet Fanny!
Whose heart goes fluttering for you every where,
Nor, when away you roam,
Dare keep its wretched home,
Love, love alone, his pains severe and many:

Then, loveliest! Keep me free,
From torturing jealousy.

VII

Ah, if you prize my subdued soul above
  The poor, the fading, brief, pride of an hour;
Let none profane my Holy See of love,
    Or with a rude hand break
    The sacramental cake:
Let none else touch the just new-budded flower;
      If not – may my eyes close,
      Love! on their lost repose.

Love or death, his options starkly stated once more – but with a new desperation born of his illness. This is manipulative, unfairly bargaining her chastity with his life. Fanny was nineteen years old, and enjoyed going to dances. She was secretly engaged to a penniless poet, currently bed-ridden by a serious illness. And so the poet's fertile brain, now fixed on love and subdued by disease, turns in on itself, his heart consumed by jealousy as his body was by disease.

Keats probably feared the worst, but hoped for the best in the weeks following his first haemorrhage. He wrote to Fanny towards the end of February, 'Do you hear the [thrush] singing over the field?' A bird's song from those fields had once been occasion for poetry, now it is a symbol of hope to share with his beloved: 'I think it is a sign of mild weather – so much the better for me.' And to James Rice (also consumptive), he exclaimed a week before, 'How astonishingly does the chance of leaving the world impress a sense of its natural beauties on us... I muse with the greatest affection on every flower I have known from my infancy... they are connected with the most thoughtless and happiest moments of our Lives... The simple flowers of our [spring] are what I want to see again.' Such beauties had once offered material for poetic depiction, but now life, love, nature, spring, summer, simplicity were what the dying man longed to experience beyond his sick-room prison.

Although preoccupied with living and loving, Keats hadn't quite turned his back on his life as a poet. He had his new collection, *Lamia, Isabella, The Eve of St Agnes and Other Poems*, to see through to publication. As his strength returned fitfully with a final spring, he began to take more interest in revising these poems for print. In early May 'La Belle Dame Sans Merci', the ballad he had written the year before, appeared under a pseudonym in Hunt's other journal *The Indicator*. The poem's sinister vision of male ensnarement amid a wintry wasteland where 'no birds sing' must have caused some rueful reflections in the jealous poet, who now delighted most in birdsong as a hopeful herald of spring.

Hunt was in fact Keats's neighbour again. Brown had let his half of the house once more, forcing Keats to find a new home. Hunt was living in Kentish Town, a north London suburb, and he suggested Keats live close by. This removed the poet from Fanny, and increased his jealous imaginings. Yet he faced a more distressing prospect still, when a trip to Italy was proposed as the only sure hope of his full recovery. Stuck in rain-drenched Devon three springs before, he had wondered why anyone would live in such a country 'when there is such a place as Italy'. Yet, now it was a necessity, Keats shrank from the prospect. Hampstead and the bosom of his beloved was where he imagined happiness, and there he longed to be.

Keats had continued to mend slowly in body, if not in his mind, as spring turned to summer, but in late June another haemorrhage struck. He was at Hunt's house, and Hunt's doctor who attended Keats advised him against continuing to live alone. Hunt offered him a room in his already overflowing house (he had five children), and Keats moved in the next day. A week later Keats's final volume of poems appeared, and was, on the whole, received more positively by critics. The sales were, however, 'very slow'. Keats had referred to *Lamia*, etc. as his 'last trial; not succeeding, I shall try what I can do in the Apothecary line'. Even that ironic hope was absurdly sanguine, as the former healer increasingly reverted to the role of desperate patient.

Staying at Hunt's was never a satisfactory set-up, but Keats had no choice. He was penniless, and felt increasingly alienated from the world of living people. His love was a source of torment rather than a comfort. In a letter from mid-August 1820 he hurled Hamlet's embittered words to Ophelia at Fanny, raging 'Go to a Nunnery, go, go!', and adopted the Dane's misanthropic outlook, declaring how he hated 'men and women more', and how he was 'glad there was such a thing as the grave'. Yet he ended this letter, his last to Fanny, with one final, qualified, hope: 'I wish I was either in your [arms] full of faith, or that a Thunder bolt would strike me.' He got his wish almost immediately.

A few days later, a letter from Fanny was misplaced and opened by one of Hunt's servants. Keats was so enraged at this violation of his privacy that he left Hunt's house immediately. He set off to Hampstead, hoping to stay at his former lodging at Well Walk, but made it as far as Wentworth Place, where Mrs Brawne offered him a safe haven. He now lived with his lover, a situation that would have been impossible had he been well. Fanny's mother was aware of their attachment, liked Keats personally, but saw no hope in his prospects. A dying, penniless poet presented little hope, but also little risk. It was human charity that allowed the doomed lovers to be together in the few short weeks before Keats's departure to Italy.

Keats left Hampstead, bound for Rome via Naples, on 13th September 1820. His ship, the *Mary Crowther*, would embark shortly from Gravesend, and Keats had a few last preparations to make in London. He had hoped Brown would accompany him, and wrote to him in Scotland, but without reply. And so, Joseph Severn, whom he had known since he was a student, stepped in at the very last minute when it looked like Keats would have to make the trip alone. Severn was a painter, whose sojourn in Rome would take him to the artistic capital of the world. (Severn would spend much of his life in Rome; he served as consul from 1861, and always acknowledged that his position and later his fame was due to the poet who died in his arms, and next to whom he would be buried sixty years later.) Severn's devotion to Keats over the last months, weeks and days of his life was exemplary, as gratifying in its untiring selflessness as the details of what this entailed are harrowing.

Reaching Rome was an ordeal from first to last. Keats had no desire to go but bowed to the advice and kindness of others. Yet in reality the trip to Rome – the four-week sea-crossing delayed because of still weather, then perilous due to stormy; the close confined quarters, cooped up with another consumptive patient on a similarly desperate bid for winter mildness; the ten further days spent in quarantine in the Bay of Naples; not to mention the emotional upheaval and distress at being parted from his loved ones – is more likely to have hastened his end. His physician in Rome even admitted as much, by which time it was far too late. Keats saw little of the Italy that was supposed to save his life.

He was put under the care of James, later Sir James Clark, who arranged for Keats to live just opposite his own house, on the Piazza di Spagna, an area known for its English residents. Invalid and companion arrived there on 17th November, nearly two months after leaving London. In the first weeks in Rome, Keats was still able to go for walks or rides in the vicinity, and Severn was able to visit galleries and ruins, and make sketches for the paintings he planned to execute while in this city of art. Yet this period was short lived, and as winter progressed, so Keats declined, demanding constant care from his companion. Dr Clark believed Keats was suffering from a stomach rather than a lung disorder, exacerbated by something on his mind. He was right about the last part at least. Keats had written to Brown from Naples how 'the persuasion that I shall see [Fanny] no more will kill me… I can bear to die – I cannot bear to leave her. Oh, God! God! God! Every thing I have in my trunks that reminds me of her goes through me like a spear… If I had any chance of recovery, this passion would kill me.' A final letter from her that arrived in his last weeks remained unopened; he couldn't bear even to see her handwriting.

More than two months before his actual death, Keats made his formal leave-taking in a final letter to Brown dated 30th November 1820:

> I have an habitual feeling of my real life having past, and that I am leading a posthumous existence… I am so weak (in mind) that I cannot bear the sight of any hand writing of a friend I love so much as I do you… There is one thought enough to kill me – I have been well, healthy, alert &c, walking with her – and now [the contrast is too painful]… I am well disappointed in hearing good news from George, – for it runs in my head we shall all die young… Remember me to all friends… Write George as soon as you receive this… and also a note to my sister – who walks about my imagination like a ghost – she is so like Tom. I can scarcely bid you good bye even in a letter. I always made an awkward bow.
>
> God bless you! John Keats.

Living a posthumous existence his thoughts now turn to oblivion, to rest and silence. The progress of his decline, detailed by Severn in his increasingly incoherent letters (he was getting little sleep through his watchful care of his dying friend), make for harrowing reading. In his final days Keats, who was experienced in these matters, asked him: '"did you ever see any one die" no – "well then I pity you poor Severn – what trouble and danger you have got into for me – now you must be firm for it will not last long – I shall soon be laid in the quiet grave – O!

I can feel the cold earth upon me – the daisies growing over me – O for this quiet – it will be my first."' It came finally on 23rd February, at 11 p.m., Keats dying quietly in his friend's arms. When his body was examined the doctors marvelled that he had survived so long. The anonymous grave, the spring flowers, the quiet earth received him three days later.

A House in Rome

The Piazza di Spagna is now one of the busiest destinations in modern Rome. Tour parties disgorge and reconvene here, and noisy groups throng the 'Spanish Steps', crowding close to the room where a young man, far from home, breathed his last. On the outside wall of that room just above their heads is a plaque declaring, 'The young English poet John Keats died in this house on the 24th February 1821 aged 25.'

Few places are as moving as that small tomb-like room in Rome. And few offer such a stark contrast between an interior – still, darkened, contemplative, heavy with the pall of memorial significance – and the uproar of the vain, fretful sunlit world immediately beyond. The room is now part of a museum to the poet's memory (shared with Shelley and Byron, who are also strongly associated with Italy). Shelley, who wrote an elegy to Keats, 'Adonais' (1821), depicting him as a poetic martyr destroyed by his critics, would also die in Italy, scarcely a year after Keats, in a boating accident, aged twenty-nine. He was washed ashore with a copy of Keats's poems open in his pocket. Shelley is also buried in the Protestant Cemetery, consolidating its significance as a shrine to English Romantic poetry, and the archetype of the wayward genius dying young. In 1877, Oscar Wilde, while still a student, visited Keats's grave and declared it 'the holiest place in Rome'. As his poem 'The Grave of Keats' puts it: 'The youngest of the martyrs here is lain, / Fair as

Sebastian and as early slain.' In a much better poem, 'On the Sale by Auction of Keats's Love Letters' (1886), Wilde compared the commercial desecration of Keats's most sacred sentiments to the degradation of the martyred Christ:

> *Is it not said that many years ago,*
> *   In a far Eastern town, some soldiers ran*
> *   With torches through the midnight, and began*
> *To wrangle for mean raiment, and to throw*
> *   Dice for the garments of a wretched man,*
> *Not knowing the God's wonder, or his woe!*

Wilde's worship of Keats occurred as his reputation was conclusively rescued from oblivion, and his poetic legacy formed. Wilde, who was busily fashioning himself as an apostle of beauty and chief spokesman for the Aesthetic Movement, found in Keats a forerunner of these ideals. Had not Keats declared towards the end that he had 'worshipped the principle of beauty in all things'? Not just in art, but in life (a central Aesthetic tenet). And had he not written a sonnet on the colour 'Blue' – a little-known, hastily composed poem that Wilde discussed in a lecture in 1884, hailing Keats as the first Aesthete?

> *Blue! 'Tis the life of heaven, – the domain*
> *   Of Cynthia, – the wide palace of the sun, –*
> *The tent of Hesperus, and all his train, –*
> *   The bosomer of clouds, gold, grey and dun.*
> *Blue! 'Tis the life of waters: – Ocean*
> *   And all its vassal streams, pools numberless,*
> *May rage, and foam and fret but never can*
> *   Subside, if not to dark blue nativeness.*
> *Blue! Gentle cousin of the forest-green,*
> *   Married to green in all the sweetest flowers, –*
> *Forget-me-not, – the Blue bell, – and that Queen*
> *   Of secrecy, the Violet: what strange powers*

Hast thou, as a mere shadow! But how great,
When in an Eye thou art, alive with fate!

And so it was that Keats, emulated by the early Tennyson, brought to vivid or dreamy life by the Pre-Raphaelite then the Symbolist painters, and now hailed as the martyred Aesthete, persecuted by the philistine hordes unready for his exquisite visions of sensual beauty, came finally to take his place in the poetic pantheon. This defining reclamation helped form his enduring legacy, and persists stubbornly today despite recent revisionist readings. The Keats of philosophical complexity and intellectual rigour has rightly been stressed as counterweight to the sybaritic celebrant of sensation. His poems, and especially the Odes, exemplify the teasing ambiguity he espoused in his concept of 'negative capability', and so deliver on the demands of a modern literary theory, obsessed with artful ambivalence. And more recently his political engagement has been stressed to challenge the myth of Keats the escapist aesthete.

And so Keats remains relevant to another generation of literary critics. Keats's verse was not divorced from the turbulent times he lived through, nor was his famous sensibility un-associated with his strongly held liberal convictions. His verse is not a chocolate box of exquisite sensuality; yet nor is it quite a soap box either. Keats had little time for didactic verse, declaring 'we hate poetry that has a palpable design upon us'. He would no doubt be equally wary of our own designs on his. The most distinctive and abiding characteristic of Keats's whole oeuvre and pronounced aesthetic is the worship of beauty. This ideal encouraged him to explore forms, feelings and sensations with an intense, and to use his word, 'disinterested', single-minded-ness. It is this that principally defines what makes Keats unique, important and influential. He was surely the first and greatest to turn feeling, free of didactic intent or some overt moral purpose, into well-wrought lyrical beauty, into 'Luxurient song', as Yeats put it. This is his enduring legacy.

Both Grave and House in Rome are still sites of pilgrimage. The visitors' book for what is now the Keats-Shelley House museum, dating back a hundred years, reveals that Keats is something of a hero around the globe, and especially with young people. It is not difficult to see why. He sang of life's pleasures and pains with equal intensity, bursting joy's grape with an hedonistic fervour that speaks eloquently of the bittersweet experience of youth. And whilst modern literary historians have rejected the tag of 'martyr', there is still a strong attraction to this idea in the popular mind. We will always need martyrs, iconic iconoclasts who embody the hopes and ideals of generations, and invariably die just as they reach their prime. In July 1969, Mick Jagger opened the Rolling Stones' free concert in Hyde Park by reading a passage from Shelley's elegy for Keats.

> *Peace, peace! He is not dead, he doth not sleep –*
> *He hath awakened from the dream of life –*

This reading was in memory of Brian Jones, the former Stones guitarist who had died two days before, aged twenty-seven. 'He is not dead', the basis for our most powerful myths, in religion, romanticism or rock. From Chatterton, Keats and Shelley, to James Dean, Brian Jones, Jim Morrison or Kurt Cobain, such figures fulfil an important collective need.

Keats was not snuffed out by an article; but the forces that stood behind that article – an establishment that attempted to preserve privilege and an ancient university education as preconditions of poetic success – undoubtedly denied him the recognition he strove for all his short life. If Keats is a 'political' poet, then this is attested in what he achieved as much as what he wrote. That the son of an ostler, who left school at fourteen, was denied the privileges of his poetic peers, who travelled on the outside of coaches to save money, and could afford to live in Italy only when he was already dead, dared to attempt what was posthumously granted to him, against time and against the odds.

The true Promethean of his generation, the fire he stole was further from his grasp, making his achievement the more wonderful, his example the more inspiring. It is not surprising that he bears the martyr's brand along with his ever-green poet's laurels.

List of works

Bibliography of sources and selected further reading

Principal sources used to prepare this biography include:

The Letters of John Keats, 1814–1821, in two volumes, edited by Hyder Edward Rollins (Cambridge, MA: Harvard University Press, 1958). This is the essential place to go to understand Keats the man, and is an invaluable resource for understanding the development of his art, and the aesthetic theories he demonstrated in his verse. They are also a rich and rewarding read in their own right.

Keats: The Critical Heritage, edited by G.M. Matthews (London: Routledge & Kegan Paul, 1971). This provides essential excerpts from the earliest reviews and views of Keats, including the infamous hostile reviews of *Endymion*.

The Keats Circle: Letters and papers and more letters and poems of the Keats circle, 2nd edition, in two volumes, edited by Hyder Edward Rollins (Cambridge MA: Harvard University Press, 1965). This is an essential resource of memoirs and recollections of the poet by his friends and family, including Charles Cowden Clarke's account of his school days and apprenticeship; Charles Brown's of their Scottish tour, and the period when they were housemates; and Severn's record of Keats's last months alive.

The Poetical Works of John Keats, edited by H. Buxton Forman (London: Oxford University Press, 1929).

John Keats, the Complete Poems, edited by John Barnard (Harmondsworth: Penguin, 1976).

John Keats, Selected Poems, edited by John Barnard (Harmondsworth: Penguin, 2007).

Keats, Robert Gittings (Harmondsworth: Penguin, 1971). This is an excellent and influential biography of Keats, which is now sadly out of print.

Keats, Andrew Motion (London: Faber & Faber, 1997). This is the most important modern biography of the poet, written by the recent Poet Laureate. It is a revisionist account of the poet, which replaces the sensitive escapist aesthete celebrated by the Victorians, with a more robust and politically engaged poet.

Posthumous Keats: A Personal biography, Stanley Plumly (New York: W.W. Norton, 2008), is an unconventional but illuminating and beautifully written recent meditation on the poet's life.

Romantics, Rebels and Reactionaries, Marilyn Butler (Oxford: Oxford University Press, 1981).

The Cambridge Companion to Keats, edited by Susan J. Wolfson (Cambridge: Cambridge University Press, 2001).

Acknowledgements

I'd like to thank the following for their help, advice and (in the case of Katy and Mark) home-made Limoncello in the preparation of this biography:

Catherine Payling of the Keats-Shelley House, Rome (www.keats-shelley.co.uk), for her kindness, help and conversation; Katy and Mark Menhinick and the cats for their Roman hospitality; Sarah Adam for the Gittings and suggestions.

Thanks to Jenny Rayner and Ellie Robins at Hesperus, and Michael Henry for his advice.

Biographical note

Robert Mighall is a former research fellow in English literature from Merton College, Oxford, and the former editor of the Penguin Classics series. He has edited and introduced a number of titles in the series, including Oscar Wilde's *The Picture of Dorian Gray* and Robert Louis Stevenson's *Strange Case of Doctor Jekyll and Mr Hyde*. He is the author of *A Geography of Victorian Gothic Fiction* (OUP, 1999), and *Sunshine* (John Murray, 2008), a cultural history of why we love the sun.